Real Cardiff

the greater city **Two**

peter finch

seren

Seren is the book imprint of
Poetry Wales Press Ltd
Nolton Street, Bridgend, Wales
www.seren-books.com

ISBN 1-85411-384-4

A CIP record for this title is available from
the British Library

The publisher works with the financial assistance
of the Welsh Books Council.

Printed by CPD (Wales), Ebbw Vale.

Some earlier versions of parts of this book
have appeared in various numbers of *Planet*,
New Welsh Review, the Institute of Welsh Affair's journal *Agenda*,
in Francesca Rhydderch's anthology, *Cardiff Central*
(Gomer Press, 2003), and on the
Muse Apprentice Guild and BBC Wales websites.
Larger sections appear as part of the Peter Finch Archive
at www.peterfinch.co.uk.

For Sue.

CONTENTS

PREFACE

Cardiff is much bigger than I thought and I've lived here all my life. *Real Cardiff* #1 with its tales of lost rivers, Roman forts, holy wells, itinerant poets, islands, castles, pubs and parks simply scratched the surface. A second volume demanded to be written. My first idea was to write a sort of Real Greater Cardiff, taking the city out to places it hasn't yet reached. But when I got to them – Creigiau, Pontprennau, Tinkinswood, Llanedeyrn – I found that they were mostly Cardiff already. The City grows by stealth.

As ever my method was to research, check the maps, then visit. If I could manage this in the company of a local then so much the better. If I couldn't then I'd talk to people I bumped into or sought out. Telling those you meet that you are writing a book opens dozens of doors. Everyone wants their story told, their take on the world recorded. Some visits were more difficult than others. Visiting Creigiau in the blinding rain to hunt for cromlechs. Getting lost on my bike in Pentwyn. Failing to conclusively find the Canna. Others were an obsessive's delight. Finding sections of the Town Walls still extant. Discovering traces of pirates in Llanrumney. Walking where Bute did, up the East Dock and down where the West used to be. In Penarth they determinedly told me that I was *not* in Cardiff. In Pontprennau that I was. In Sully they didn't know.

There were a lot of pubs too. Old ones. Full of beer, baps and poets. I need to thank some of my walking companions – the photographer John Briggs, the architect Jonathan Adams, the author Tom Davies, political activist John Osmond, poet Grahame Davies, webmeister Viv Goldberg, angel maker Morgan Francis. Mick Felton and the staff at Seren fed me ideas. You need to visit Queen Street Station. Did that. And the ski slope. Next time. My book-dealing friend Alan Beynon again unearthed old photos, and ancient maps. Two public art commissions – one for a poem on BT's west Cardiff Internet Data Centre and another for a text to top the Lamby Way landfill – provided entrees to places I would not otherwise have had access. John Williams, Ifor Thomas, Huw Thomas, Wiard Sterk, Dave Coombs, and others are to be thanked for their suggestions and, often, simply for listening to me. Ceri Black for helping me locate Billy the Seal. David Lloyd for pointing me at Cardiff, NY. Mike Donleavy gave me access to his late father, Alderman Phil Donleavy's papers, for which I am extremely grateful.

Greatest thanks have to be given to Sue who read everything, twice, three times, went to sleep over it, red penned it, gave it a score, suggested bits I should scrap, told me when I wasn't making sense or had got just too boring for words. She came on the visits, drank in the pubs, waited patiently while I climbed up through trees, ducked into alleyways or disappeared down roads I'd never visited before.

If you've come upon this book first and not yet read *Real Cardiff* #1 then I commend that volume to you. I'd say that, wouldn't I, but I believe it too. It's been updated and recently re-issued. *Real Cardiff*, Real Kardiff. The whole deal is there. The Finch *Real Cardiff* website at www.peterfinch.co.uk/cardiff is the place for further discoveries. There's text and photography online there that is in neither volume.

The present book, of course, is not supposed to be read straight through. It's no novel and there's no sequential plot. You dip. You follow your interests. Check out where you live, if it's here. Write to me and complain if it's not.

Out of the window right now there is a blue sky with a few Magritte-like clouds. Not bad for cool April. It rains a lot here but not always. Cardiff by the Severn estuary, looking out to the deep Atlantic. Three thousand uninterrupted miles until you get to anywhere else.

                                                        Peter Finch
                                                Roath, April, 2004

INTRODUCTION

CARDIFF: WALES BEHIND IT, EUROPE IN FRONT

There's more rain, sheets of it, coming in from the south west and pouring up Queen Street. The pedestrians are mostly half clad and trying to ignore it. Style but no grace. This is Friday night and the capital is doing what it usually does. Celebrating the present. Living in the hedonistic moment and doing it for all it's worth. Reports that Cardiff consumes on average 60% more alcohol per head of population than anywhere else in the UK might not look that realistic in the suburbs on a Saturday morning but they do along St Mary Street at 2.30 am most nights when the clubs disgorge. Cardiff Fun City. Business Centre. Empire of the stable, and the senseless.

The city has been the Welsh capital now for more than fifty years but only in the last ten has it really begun to show it. Drinks Capital, Sports Capital, Service Capital, Call Centre Capital, Shopping Capital, Capital of fast cars and media businesses, Capital of the creative arts. "Culture is now our core business," said Russell Goodway, former Council Leader and one-time Lord Mayor, although nobody really knew just what that meant.

Cardiff never made it as EU Capital of Culture for 2008, although it bid hard. Other contenders were bigger. Liverpool, another post-industrial port with a multi-cultural hinterland and the city which won, is enormous by comparison[1]. Cardiff doesn't connect with its Valleys. The Valleys which gave the city its industrial existence. Rhondda. Taff. Rumney. Their populations flock here for the glitter of Cardiff's shops and the gleam of its bars. They run our service industries, manage our call centres. Do we do anything for them? We take their cash.

Cardiff, which began as a sliver of a medieval town, clustered inside town walls, south of the Castle, east of the Taff river, is now an extended lozenge. It's built into the elongated space that lies north of the sea and south of the ridges that mark the beginnings of the coal field. Cardiff squeezes east through Trowbridge, Pentwyn and Pontprennau to threaten Newport. Pushes west through Ely, St Fagans and Creigiau to look in the eye of Swansea. Strip developed. Hanging round the rail link for warmth. It can take a good forty minutes to drive across – chicaned and bus laned. Traffic lights at every super-store. Nowhere else in Wales comes anywhere near us.[2]

As a city Cardiff is new. Other than the Castle and a few churches there's little extant that pre-dates Victoria. Until the industrial revolution Cardiff wasn't much more than a sixth-rate market town with a silt-threatened quay and a reputation for ruffians and occasional fishing. 1800 years of languishing on the way to somewhere else[3] has left us little exploitable history. The coal and iron explosion of the early nineteenth century made Cardiff expand like a balloon. The Bute family, above all others, held sway: land owners, transport developers, dock builders, pre-eminent exploiters of trade. They were in charge for more than a hundred years.

By the time the boom was all over and industry in rapid decline the population had risen by more than 250,000, sucking in immigrants from all over Wales, from Ireland, the West Country, and beyond. We lived in Victorian terraces or slumland back-to-backs. The streets were dark. Cardiff, leading coal exporter of the world, five docks, a hundred warehouses and endless rail yards, sat, smelling of the steel works, in the unending Welsh rain.

World cities had long pasts, great ancient buildings, planned early redevelopments, trappings of Empire, might and power. Cardiff had St John's Church, the Castle, Splott and Grange farmhouses and a monument to a great ancient tree which once stood at Fairoak. Stump is still there, top of Ty Draw Road, go take a look.

There were other things too. Buildings, factories, industrial enterprises, stretches of regal space which we could have honoured. But mostly we knocked them flat. The Georgian Town Hall on its island in the middle of High Street; the Victorian Town Hall with its monumental columns lining St Mary Street; the Cardiff Arms Hotel sitting at right angles across Castle Street; the great Park Hall Cinema and Theatre, now a car park; the medieval Town Walls, now a couple of metres back of Bradford & Bingley; Bethel Chapel, later the Casablanca Club, in Mount Stuart Square, now an open space; the perfect termination of Georgianesque Windsor Place in the arc of St Andrews Crescent, now wrenched apart by Boulevard de Nantes and its four lane traffic; Hills Drydock; the Rhymney Rail Station; the Canal which made parts of Cardiff look like Amsterdam; the Missions to Seamen; The Mariners Church on the West Dock Basin; the Custom House, the North and South, the New Sea Lock, the Glastonbury Arms, the Greyhound, the Rainbow Club, the Cape Horn Hotel, the Peel Street Mosque.

These things have gone and, for the most part, are now
unremarked in the landscape. No plaques or signs. There was one on
the Town Wall but it's been taken down. Look them up in *Cardiff in
Old Photographs*. Should Cardiff have redeveloped itself differently?
Or are these memories of past places merely nostalgia? Cities should
not be museums. Some things will inevitably be in the way, others will
fall down. Cardiff's history has been badly served by the rush of the
late twentieth century. The gallop for profit has given us new bars and
apartments to be proud of. The lights of Cardiff Bay now shine all the
way over to Bristol. Snow domes on Ferry Road. Millennium Star
Cruisers on the Arms Park. A great boulevard connects the old city
with the new. The bronzed cycle helmet of the Wales Millennium
Centre changes colour with the sky. But the past has largely been
forgotten. Cardiff is now a modern city – dense, growing, anonymous.

When I started to think about *Real Cardiff* I decided to try to walk
every street of the Capital. Phyllis Pearsall[4] did that for the *London A
to Z*, writing up her rambles along 23,000 streets on filecards and
storing them in shoe boxes under her bed. The fourth edition of the
Super Red Book of Cardiff (2001) lists a mere 7500 streets. Easy. I'd
spent a youth street walking, wasting time, getting places, returning
from distant drunken parties and learning that after two hours of
stumbling you were usually drunker than when you started. I set off.

I got to places I simply did not know existed. Fort Street,
Pembroke Terrace, King Leopold Street, Trade Street, Marionville
Gardens, Tide Fields Road. Streets named after great battles, after
political leaders, after Welsh counties, after local dignitaries, after
metals, after heavenly bodies, after places in the West of England,
friends of the developer, members of Bute's family, after the
woodlands on which they were built. And then, heading slowly east,
I came to the vastness that is Llanrumney. Stunned I gave up. I did
the rest on a bike or in a car.

Unlike its rivals Cardiff relishes its otherness. Distance and alienation; a world unknowable, full of anxiety, speed and noise. It does
not yet have the high-rise, system-build and featureless city block
look of Chicago or Birmingham where adornment, embellishment
and personalisation have been sacrificed in the face of the pulsating
hoards. But it does have anonymity and it celebrates that. You can go
from one end of Queen Street to the other on a crowded Saturday
and have no one look at you, other than charity junkies and Big Issue
sellers. You get swift service from shop assistants who never talk to

you. You can have an affair here and no one will spot you. You can commit a murder and not be caught.

But don't let's exaggerate the depersonalisation. Compared to Manchester, Birmingham or London life here is all sweetness and delicate light. A promised land of Ikea, Marks and Spencer, B&Q. And places you can actually walk to.

I'm walking now, down Lloyd George, towards the Bay. The magnet of water. In front of me is the focus: Pier Head Building, red brick with unaccountable cannons in its forecourt, dwarfed by the new buildings around it. Schizophrenic Lloyd George with its two street signs on opposite sides[5]: Lloyd George Avenue and Bute Avenue – the two makers of Wales. Along it run Persimmon's apartment blocks – Rimini, Amalfi, Sienna, Sorrento. All Italian. Behind them rises Redrow's Altolusso on Bute Terrace, 292 skyscraper apartments[6]. A new Mediterranean for Wales. Lloyd George spills out onto Roald Dahl Plass, Norwegian author, son of Cardiff. To my right, beyond the underpass graffitied as *Docks Crew 2003* is the Greek Church. Then Tŷ Gobaith, for the destitute. Cardiff, Wales behind it, Europe in front.

This is it, what we are. The youngest capital. A Merc goes past carrying the well-to-do en-route to see La Traviata. Below the street security cameras an Albanian accosts two Somalis, or maybe the other way round. Sun comes out. Cardiff is getting to be like this more and more.

notes

1. National Statistics Census 2001 shows the population of Liverpool as 439,000 and Cardiff as 305,353
2. Swansea 2001 population is 223,301. The new, first city of Wales, the City of Newport is 137,011
3. The Romans used Cardiff as a staging post on their way to Neath. In the middle-ages Carmarthen was a much bigger and more important town. Only the accident of having a navigable river quay with the iron and coal valleys leading to it allowed Cardiff to beat the much better ports of Barry and Swansea. Newport, too, might have been in the running if it hadn't been for an early failure of tramway and railway builders to exploit the routes to their natural epicentre.
4. Phyllis Pearsall (1909-1966) walked 3000 miles and worked 18 hour days in order to produce her first edition. There was no way I could compete with this.
5. Under Bay redevelopment the grand boulevard connecting Cardiff's two inner cities was to be called Bute Avenue. A commemorative plaque outside Craft in the Bay's Q Shed marks the fact. It was renamed as Lloyd George Avenue when the City took over powers from the Cardiff Bay Development Corporation.
6. *Transition, Elegance, Inspiration, Style, Passion, Imagination* are Redrow's marketing brochure descriptive keywords.

EAST

ROATH – CAPITAL OF WALES

I'm walking through Roath, the classic worker's town. Its meshed terraces spread east from the industrial city. Roath originally stretched the whole way from the Crockerton East Gate to the Rumney River. Rath. Raz. The name has a hard, pre-British sound. There's a theory, which I like enormously, that the city should never have been called Cardiff in the first place. Its original name was Roath. Ptolemy[1], the early Egyptian mathematician and geographer who compiled the first world maps from the gossip of itinerant mariners, has a place called Rathostathibios, scratched in on the papyrus, next to the Taff more or less where Cardiff Castle came to stand. Say that word a few times. Rathostathibios. You can make it sound like Roath. Like Taff. Râth-Tâv. Y Rhâth. Roth. Rov. Roath. Roath on the Taff taking in everything from the Ely to the Rumney. When the country came to be divided into parishes Cardiff, by then already a burgh, became the name for the western half and Roath for the east. The division was a matter of administrative convenience, no more than that. The Cardiff half, with its Castle, its quay and its navigable river grew in importance. Roath, with its hillfort-sited church, mill and manor house, remained a village. Until the nineteenth century, that is, when Bute's industrial expansion filled the fields between the two places with tenements and streets. Roath, capital of Wales. Could well have been.

Where Roath begins and ends today is a matter for dispute. Parts of its southern extremity have been taken over by Adamsdown, Splott, Atlantic Wharf, Tremorfa, and Pengam Green. To the north

Cathays, Penylan, Waterloo, and Plasnewydd all encroach. I've always lived in Roath. When I was a child we seemed to move every couple of years as part of some financial management scheme of my father's. He theorised that if you bought and sold judiciously you could make enough spare to get by on. Not that his schemes ever appeared to actually generate much cash. We went from Kimberly Road

to Waterloo Gardens to Ty Draw Place to Westville Road. Always
Cardiff east which my mother insisted that I either call Penylan or
Roath Park, depending on which house we happened to be in at the
time. It was the same for our brief sojourn in Canton. When we were
there I had to put Victoria Park down as the district. In later life she
actually did move to Penylan although her letters then labelled the
place as Lakeside. God knows what would have happened if she'd
made it to Lisvane. She probably wouldn't have regarded that as
Cardiff at all.

The main highway east is Newport Road. This lorry-choked
artery passes through the site of the Roath Court manor house's
gatehouse, past Cardiff's best old style Brains pub, The Royal Oak,
with its second floor boxing gym, its rock music backroom and its
heavy-booted regulars, and out onto what was once the causeway.
The flatland between here and the eastern rise of Rumney Hill was
(and still is if you peer between the tarmac) bogland. These are the
great eastern salt marshes which, before the building of the seawall,
were regularly inundated at high tide. Here was an almost East
Anglian landscape of reed, fishing henge, and drainage gully.
Salmon. Shrimp. Crab. Grass. Bladder-wrack. Today it's shopping
mall territory. Supermarkets, Drive-in Burger Bars, bathroom
warehouses, office supplies, curtains, pots with butterflies painted on
their sides, fitted kitchens, basket-weave dining suites, emulsion
paint, wooden garden ornaments, drill bits that cost £1 a dozen but
snap as soon as you put them anywhere near a wall. Newport Road
blazes out along the line of the ancient Portway[2], the Roman Road
that ran from Isca to Nidum, Caerleon to Neath. It's been here a
while, this route.

To the south the streets of Splott and Tremorfa are hampered by
a dense corrugation of speed humps that slow even the Kawasakis
that leap across them. Road deaths in poorer districts were long
thought to be the fault of addled youth spinning sparks out of the
road surface in their side-skirted, sewer-piped Peugeots and speaker-
stuffed Novas. Research has shown that they are more a product of
the amount time people here actually spend on the streets and the
number they need to cross in order to get where they are going. Still,
nothing quite like seeing a gleaming boy racer fingering his earring
as he boomboxes along at a five mph crawl. On the causeway – the
A4161 – it's a different matter. Six lanes of solid diesel doing fifty

make the proposition of walking to get anywhere terminally daunt-
ing. America has landed among the carpet superstores.You don't like
this Berber twist? Drive next door to see theirs.

I walk it anyway, sidestepping through low parking-bay walls and
between the massed transport of south Wales' Sunday shoppers. The
flat I used to rent in the last south-side terrace block of Edwardian
three-stories has now been refashioned as Dijabrindab Eerwidja, an
Asian grand residence next to where the brick works used to be. At
pub chuck out you could once hear Twist & Shout[3] roaring passed,
up along Newport Road and over towards the Harlequins. C'mon
c'mon c'mon c'mon. A song you could always sing in Cardiff when
you were drunk. I began my writing career here. Tried it as a singer
with a guitar, harmonica harness, bottle caps on my shoes, the whole
bit. I did out of tune, self-penned folk songs. Drizzle-drenched Bob
Dylan. South Wales Donovan. I was terrible. I toured the pubs. This
is what folk singers did, I'd heard. Got in the bar, scraped, clanged. I
got thrown out of everywhere. Even the scrumpy drunks in the
Greyhound[4] couldn't cope. Cun you do Nelliedean? Well sodoffthen.
So I went back to the flat and turned my awful songs into awful
poems. Time improved them. I think. I wrote Welsh Wordscape there,
pissed off with Wales' self-referential tie-wearing conservatism.
Where was the future? Somewhere else.

Roath peters out at the Rumney where the Lleici outfalls and the
once coracle-fished waters swirl dirtily into the Severn. This is the
border. Indifferently the land rises. Roath behind it. Capital of Wales.
Roath – the town that floats.

WATERLOO HILL AND THE THREE BREWERS

The road lifts almost imperceptibly towards St Margaret's Church.
Circular church yard. Sure sign of the site of a llan. Was there an
Iron-age encampment here? Maybe. Nothing proven, all supposition
and rumour. Circular church yards were often constructed on a pre-
existing religious site. A bronze-age holy place made Christian in the
dark ages. The old usurped and built on. Could have happened here.
Why else this mound at the edge of Roath Brook? Was it once topped
with a stone circle? Were there altar stones? Was there a holy spring

emerging from the blessed rock? The churchyard gate off St Margaret's Crescent is surmounted on each pillar by cut blocks with evidence of metal work within. These are re-used fragments of the first St Margaret's. This place has a long history. Its ghosts are still around.

A small, lime-washed country church served Roath village for hundreds of years. Records from the twelfth century show a chancel here. Bishop Kitchen, the man who sold off most of Llandaf's wealth at the time of the Reformation, lists a Chapel of Ease on this site. Roath – a scattering of souls. Coracle fishermen. Farmers. But by the mid-nineteenth century Roath had grown. The old church, which had served Dean's Farm, Ty Mawr, Roath Court House and a scattering of cottages, was pulled down and replaced. Bute had a hand in it. His family mausoleum had been erected as an outbuilding to the country church in 1800. The body of the first Marquess along with those of both his wives and his eldest son were interred here. In 1867, his grandson, the third Marquess put up the money to rebuild both his family mausoleum and the church, the one as a consequence of the other. This was the height of the Victorian era. Cardiff was a boom town. Money was passing through the hands of the rich in golden streams. Alexander Roos, architect to the Bute estate, designed a church with a spire on the south-west corner. Foundations were dug. Walls were marked out. But Roos didn't last. In 1868 Bute appointed the great church architect, John Pritchard, in his stead. Pritchard's cruciform design, reusing Roos' foundations, opened later the same year. No corner spire but instead a central tower. Solid glory in heavy

stone. The new building now sits where its white painted predecessor once did. Much larger, it engulfs the ghost shape of the country church like a space ship from Mars.

But not all has shifted. The giant yew which overhung the first church is still in place. The sgate through which I enter the churchyard is where there was once a stile. The path is where it always was. The ground rolls

slowly west to the wooden lych gate[5] set precisely on the spot of its predecessor. The service in progress as I pass leaks out through a scratchy speaker. The Lord praised to a congregation of squirrels, hedgehogs and birds.

In the 1970s the churchyard was largely cleared of memorials. Style of the time. The half a dozen or so that remain are supposed to convey the spirit of what was once here. Stone lozenges. Granite flags. The grass mowers can zoom between them. Haven for drunks – but they hardly ever come. Once or twice a sleeping bag under the yew or in the porch. Occasionally children playing football. Mostly the place stays still. Facing west, looking out of the church's north transept is the country church's original window. It's the one you can see in photographs of that structure taken in the 1860s. Still here, lifted in one piece and incorporated into Pritchard's splendid new structure. Light pours through it, as it has done for centuries. Like God, the past carrying on.

Bute's Mausoleum, upgraded in 1881, is unexpectedly stark and severe. Seven sarcophagi in Red Peterhead granite lie polished and unadorned. The mortal remains of seven Butes are here, above the surface, hard-cased in tombs like the Tsars in St Petersburg. Chill cold and oh so formal and so many miles from their place of birth. The mausoleum sits behind a gilded wrought-iron screen. It looks like Egypt in there, the set of a B movie where ghouls and mummies spin around corners and spirits rise from the very stones.

Beyond the church I cross where the ditches, reens and minor branches of the Lleici once flowed. Waterloo Gardens, home of well-tended flower beds and summer silver bands. The famous hut, now demolished, that held Dannie Abse's engraved initials. And once, tennis courts, now lawn. Toddlers chase balls across it. Terriers return thrown sticks to their bench seated owners. At night youths climb the spear-headed railings for drink and dope. Syringes left in the flowerbeds. Trees broken. Seats smashed. Waterloo Gardens – Keeper's hut abandoned to save cash – last bastion of the manicured lawn and pruned rose – slowly sliding towards inner-city loss.

I skirt the traffic calmers, patrolled in the day by yellow-clad cross-ing wardens, guarding the child route to Marlborough School, waving to mothers, helping those more aged than themselves to cross the road. This is now the heart of Roath Village – moved north from the earlier cluster around the Court and the Church[6]. Corner shop, butcher, hairdresser reusing the old dairy, post office. Once this was all Deri Farm, ditch-drained wet land, the high reach of the tide fields, Bristol Channel salt in the soil, just a touch.

The Lleici took many routes through here. Its tributaries are dried now, culverted, gone. The Mill which stood across Sandringham Road and had its wheel in the brook near the junction with Trafalgar Road was pulled down at the time of Victoria's jubilee. The leat left drained and abandoned. The ford rebuilt as a bridge. Waterloo Road rises. This is still Roath, just, right where Penylan begins. The council once tried to reclassify the whole area as Waterloo – a new district for the geographically uncertain – didn't work.

I climb passed the long terrace which overlooks Mill Gardens – parts of the stone wheel housing still visible among the trees. This was the Goosler – free land run with the animals of small-holders – pigs, geese. Shit enriching the soil through long centuries – now used to grow shrub and short grass. Kids on bikes. Anoraked adults, hands behind backs, out running dogs.

Flash, timid ginger tom, lead shot pellets found embedded in his back, would have crossed here as he made his break for freedom when his owners moved from one street to the next. For a time the neighbourhood was plastered with LOST CAT posters and false sightings were legion. Tried checking the lanes at dusk, crepuscular roaming time, calling. Saw nothing. Cats don't use human pathways. They slide below shrubbery and drift along the tops of walls. Flash appeared three weeks later, half dead[7], on the Penylan allotments, broken paw, labelled collar intact. A gardener brought him back in a plastic bag, hanging from the handlebars of his bike.

Above the park, houses now steam along the Taff Vale Roath Dock Branch line where pannier-tanked steam-trains once dragged coal to be offloaded and exported through Bute's great port. This is almost the district's final expansion. Waterloo Gate. A late house cluster infill – classless Vectras on the drive, 4x4s, Fiestas. Who lives here? Retirees. Young professionals. Urban neatness. Brookside.

Past Gwyneth Lewis' house I turn into Melrose Avenue and sink down towards the pub. Melrose is all semis, 50s pebble-dash terraces, metal windows. The road car parked herringbone style. There's no longer space for everyone's van and Vauxhall right outside their doors. This is still Roath, still Penylan. The slope runs to the site of the old brickworks at the hill's foot, the place that produced the hard-sided red imperial bricks from which most of this district was built. Still tough as hell to get a drill into. Black mortar holds them together. Has done so since the late 1800s. Will do for some time yet. This mortar, made out of ash from the steelworks, holds more moisture than present day mixes. Breathes and moves. Houses here have yet to fall down.

The Three Brewers, at the foot of the hill, is a brick and concrete slab of a tavern – multi-story car park, sixties high rise architecture – tough and unwelcoming. There's been an attempt at softening with the addition of outdoor benches and umbrellas on the forecourt and sloping grass. The clientele drink lager here. Earrings. Track suits. Tattoos. The brewery's signs label this A SIZZLING PUB – SUMMER FUN EVERY WEEKEND. No past, endless present. The upstairs bar where you can usually get a seat is closed. I contemplate the reality TV bedlam of the ground floor. Bright yellow light. Hip hop at murderous decibel. The older comfort of the New Dock Tavern lies twenty minutes back the way I've come. Do I? I do.

LAMBY WAY

South east of the city on the far bank of the Rumney where the land once slid furtively into the grey sea stands a low mound. This promi-nence too has the air of the hill fort about it, rounded, rough green, unbuilt on. But these are the Lamby Moors, part of the great salt-marsh levels that run from here to the Usk. Nothing higher than a horse. Fen land. A sea that encroaches, a coast that ebbs and flows with the tide. Yet all is not what it seems. This is actually the City of Cardiff Lamby Way landfill site. The new age hill fort is a renovated heap of refuse. It is compacted, layered with impervious liner, capped with several meters of soil, and planted with grass, ground cover, alder, periwinkle, hawthorn. Below it the Rumney meanders to the sea, the mud flats moulder, sea borne flotsam beaches on a shore of gash brick and abandoned hard core. Two tides of refuse meet where the reeds still grow and the gulls swarm in a marauding spiral.

When Cardiff was a town of less than 2000 inhabitants, a situation it had been in from at least the Romans to the industrial revolution, refuse was largely left in the streets. There was a heap next to the Castle, near the North Gate, which

used to wash into the Rose and Crown when it rained. There was another by St John's Church. One by the Cross in St Mary Street and a great heap outside the South Gate. These were mounds of night soil, animal carcass, waste cloth, and fat scrapings taken there by scavenger cart. No paper, no packaging, no tins, no bottles, no junked furniture, no outmoded computers and bust fax machines, no failed kettles, no doorless fridges, no bed bases, no mattresses, no cracked phones, no polystyrene packaging, no polyurethane, no polypropylene, no polythene, no bri-nylon, no plastic. Pre-industrial waste was minimal. The poor re-used everything. Today we are rich and we don't. We dump. We take it to the shores of the mud-cased Rumney. We bury it at Lamby Way (South) where the land is too weak to support housing, where the farms produce turf, where there are dogs and paddocks, where the city ends.

I'm visiting with Wiard Sterk, the Dutch-born commissions director for CBAT, the Arts & Regeneration Agency. They are managing *Breathing In Time Out*, an art project focusing on waste management, landfill and sustainable power generation. The funding comes from the state, from Hyder's inheritor, Western Power, and from nearby Tesco. The lead artist is Jeroen van Westen[8]. They need words, somewhere. I'm looking. I've been here before, of course, on Lamby Way Open Day, in full sun, where the dust-cart car-park is decked like a Church bazaar with stalls selling tea, crisps, potted plants, and gardening equipment. There are tours of the re-cycling shed and an opportunity to buy bargain-priced compost bins. A man dressed as a giant green plastic bottle wanders around encouraging everyone to

green-bag recycle rather than chuck. You can get tea. There's a demonstration of potting-compost mixing and an air of renewal, reuse, sustainability, and self-sufficiency. People come on bikes. Walk in from Rumney with the dog on a lead. Kids play ball. You can't smell anything foul. Can I see the dump itself? Sorry, far too dangerous.

This time it's different. We are met by Colin Crooks, an engineer on secondment from Northern Ireland, and keen to show us the whole gigantic site. There's a light drizzle coming in off the sea. Anoraked, in green boots, hard hats and the obligatory luminous over-waistcoat we get into his 4x4 for the short slide across the sludge to view the reclaimed hill.

Lamby Way has been here for a decade or so, taking the content of Cardiff's lanes in black plastic and using them to build the incline up which we now climb. The ground is rough but green, crossed by fences built to catch the discarded polythene which blows from the adjacent active landfill cell. Colin's talk is full of birds, waves of gulls followed by crows, foxes, squirrels, a cormorant, a flight of Canada geese, skylark. The methane generated by the waste decomposing beneath our feet is taken off through a grid of pipes. You can see their metal capped manifolds set right across the site. The gas feeds three power generators which in turn put electricity back into the National grid. In technical terms this is a gas-recovery system with enclosed flaring. It's good. It saves money. It cuts the smell. At the hilltop there's a new lake, unnamed, an overflow stream and an unrivalled view west into the city. The horizon lines with the centre's high-rises, Capital Tower, Brunel House, the Churchill Way apartment blocks. Designer Cardiff, European Capital, no smog. But there is rain, o yes. There's nothing to stop it as it storms in from the south-West. It builds up speed, leaving southern Ireland, crossing St George's Channel. This is its first landfall. The trees we plant here have to be surrounded with plastic wind guards until they establish deep roots. Even then I have my doubts that they'll survive. There's a ragged line of damp dogwood rising behind a line of black-mesh fencing. Tussocky grass. The shores of the new lake are unplanted brown. No pathways. It will be turned into a municipal golf course, once it's done. Drive direct into a force nine. The most exposed fairway in Wales. Should be fun.

The 4x4 takes us back through the entrance yard where hoards of dust-cart drivers on break stand around drinking tea. There are dumpers and street sweepers, sludge-gulpers and hand-carts in larger number than I imagined the city owned. They enter the active landfill across a weighbridge and leave the same way. How much gets dumped defines the city's tax bill. The weighbridge is guarded by the falconer whose birds of prey patrol the landfill in an attempt to keep back the marauding gulls. But it's an unequal battle. The seabirds arrive in waves chasing new garbage deliveries. They scavenge briefly then leave, no energy lost on fruitless search through debris from which every edible trace has already been cleaned. Men forage along the dump's edges collecting blown polythene and other wind-borne debris. Drivers play jets of water onto their vehicle's wheels and undersides. They all smoke, to keep back the smell. It's there, but fainter than I'd expected. Leachate[9] sinking into the landscape, piped into the main east-west interceptor sewer which sweeps under here.

We reach the landfill's far end, beyond a third, not yet active cell. This is currently a black valley full of leachate flow controls and vent pipes, waiting for the binbags to arrive. Here stands the sea wall. Van Westen will build a public walkway past here, a track between depressing sea and reclaimed ground. A path was lost when the landfill was first established. Jeroen will put it back. The land is thick

with plant waste, decomposing vegetation collected from Cardiff's parks and woodlands. In the chill air a tractor shifts the compost into conical piles. Everything steams. There's a sea of sludge here, a pale brown blancmange surrounding the main sewer inspection shaft. Roath Park, says Colin. Lake dredgings. The soil of north Cardiff come to rest in the city's south.

Just outside the landfill, between the access road and the start of Rumney Hill is a lake, full of water birds and floating grass islands. Lamby Way (North). Reclaimed land converted to civic amenity. Pond, reed, pathways, open grass, plantings. Parc Tredelerch[10]. As a contrast to what we've recently seen and, maybe, to underline just what can be done in the name of reclamation, we visit. Three of us, still in boots, hard-hats and luminous jackets. The park is full of gypsy horses. They don't need them for work anymore, Wiard tells us. They're kept for sentiment. Gypsies have always dealt in horses and they do so still. A man in a black anorak with a terrier on a lead accosts us. You're in charge of this park, aren't you? I've just counted thirty-six horses over there eating the bushes. He gesticulates at the scrubby grass. You need to do something. Colin smiles. It's the hard-hat uniform which imparts authority. I'll make a note, he says.

The floating islands are for the birds to nest on. There are observation platforms and small piers ready for fishermen. The reeds have not yet shown significant growth, but they will. The elevated Eastern Avenue link road thrums beyond us, trains clatter along the main rail line. It's not the quietest of amenities I've visited but, for all that, it works. Damp, green, and despite everything, peaceful. Once men who fished the Rumney from coracles would have had their huts here, scratching a Cardiff living from the unending swamp. Next to Lamby Way proper there's a new industrial park accommodating light engineering and storage. They've moved a few of the drainage reens to get it built. Cors Crychydd[11]. Concrete and aluminium. White vans. Road dust.

Wiard tells me that Jeroen has planned a thirty metre long, half metre high frieze running across an entrance he has designed for the reclaimed hill. The frieze will bear words in foot high letters. A sort of stutter. Architectural. Visible from the road, from the river, from the sea. Rubbish. Recycle. Seicl. Ysbwriel. Rwbish. Ffrwcs. Ffrwcsach. Twmbwriach. Hen siabach. Sqrwtsh. Consarnach. Spwr spore rwb rub sach sack sh sh. Fflwcs. The words run through my head. I take them out and write them down. Spwr spore rw b rub sa ch sa ck sh sh gas. What is this? Rubbish, sbwriel, will enter, move, change; slowly recycle itself into nwy, into gas. The concrete approach. Like the poetry rather than the mix.

I work the words. In Welsh, faint language of these soggy lands centuries back, it's ysbwriel, frewcsach, rwbish, fflwcs. The way the

Welsh language has so much wealth fascinates me. What the hell are fflwcs? How did they arrive? Jeroen gets the versions by e-mail, makes his suggestions, then tosses them back. He wants the deal in capitals with dots at x height[12]. There's an echo of a Celtic / Roman / David Jones back-glance here but so slight you wouldn't notice.

WASTE·CYCLE·GLE·SBWRIEL·FFLWCS·BGS·BLK·WAS·A ·IS·A·BACK·AS·A·NEW·IS·NWY·GAS

Does that look like Tolkien? Like Eric Gill? It does not. How does it sound? What are these words like when they talk in the air? I find an old computer headset and read a version into my pc, get carried away by the rhythm and double its length. E-mail it to Holland. Finch spwriel-speak in the ether. Out there.

I need to pursue the fflwcs connection. What is this word? Who recognises it. Older, south east-Wales Welsh the dictionary tells me. I ask around. Results are inconclusive. I bump into Dafydd Êl[13] at an Earthfall reception at Chapter. What does he think? He offers to check. I e-mail it in. He bangs it round the Cynulliad and I get a fulsome multi-layered response by return. Fflwcs is recognised as meaning rubbish by enough people. It's a word from the south, one that would have had a currency here when Cardiff was a walled-town and the Rumney was clean and clear. Fflwcs is overgrowth, weed. The stuff a farmer would scrape as useless from his field's surface and leave to rot, to heat, to turn to gas. Weed-flowers. Phlox. The piece turns, flies between Cardiff and the Netherlands, switches, gets half-rhyme, gets discussed, gets longer, gets cut.

WASTE·CYCLE·RECYCLE·GLE··SBWRIEL··GRASS·GASH ·FFLWCS·BGS·NEW·BLK·BAGS··ISA·WSA·BACK··IS·A·NWY· NEW··IS·A··NEWGAS[14]

One x-height dot says word break, two say draw in breath. This waste hill is all spwriel. There is a gash of grass. Fflwcs in the bags. Bgs. They are compacted. The methane leachate seeps. Grows. Wsss. Isa. Wsa. Still a sort of stutter. Nwy is made new. Newgas is faster than new gas. It flames inside the generators. Power seeps back.

RUMNEY

At the foot of the Hill, far side of the Rumney River, in what was once Monmouth stands the Grade Two listed Rumney Pottery. The building, right on the edge of the river with the remains of an ancient riverside quay outside, looks much like any middle-class refurbished cottage. White pebble dash, cotoneaster over the door, gravel drive. Records show this place to have been making pots for at least five hundred years, four hundred of them by the same family.

The present potter, Robert Giles, tells me he was probably the one who was here making tea sets when I visited on a school trip in the sixties. As craftsmen his family goes back at least eight generations on this site. But he's not in awe of history. He shows me the kiln, scratching clay as he speaks. The workshop is full of unfinished ceramic work, wooden benches, pots stacked on slatted shelves, dust. Through the window I can see where the horse-powered pug mill which churned the dug clay once stood. He tells me he used to dig the clay himself, from just across the river where Magnet Joinery now stands. Gave it up. Didn't seem right excavating six foot holes in real estate which belonged to someone else. Where does the clay come from today? Some English China from Cornwall but mostly it's shipped in from Brazil. The pottery was famous in the nineteenth century for its domestic water pitchers and bread crocks and later for its Victorian wash sets and utilitarian washing pans, widely used in the mining valleys. Today work is all done on commission. Sgraffito slipware for schools, churches, golf clubs. Mugs with your name on them. Plates

with a society badge at their centre. In production during my visit is a commemorative plate for the International Association of Practice Accountants. Big dinner coming up in Cardiff. All attending guests will get one, decoratively boxed, to take home. The Pottery bestseller is a four-inch skulldish made to a special design for the band, Super Furry Animals. Can I buy one? Sorry, you'll have to talk to

them about that. It might be
old but the Rumney Pottery
stays up to date. Has its own
web presence, makes enough
living to keep a family,
welcomes visitors, doesn't
pressure them to buy too
much. The grey river slides
outside. Its mud glistens.

Across the bridge I leave the
city. Here it once finished.
Before 1938 the village of
Rumney belonged to

Monmouth. Greater Cardiff, east of the river, had yet to be built. On
the hillside my map shows an ancient monument – Rumney Castle,
Cae Castell. But there is nothing obvious to see. The map is a nineteen
eighties OS, surveyed before the great Bay development began.
Ancient monuments don't disappear, do they? According to the
records this was one of Robert Fitzhamon's[15] Welsh-subduing fortifications built on Roman foundations. Looking for its remains today is
not a simple matter. The site, I discover, was formally excavated in
1978. Coins and pottery were found, wall footings photographed,
and Norman ringworks were traced. All on land reported as "behind
the Oaklands Hotel". The gathered evidence was deposited at the
headquarters of the Glamorgan Gwent Archaeological Trust. In 1983
this building burned down. Dig reports were lost. All that remain now
are memories. And ash. The Oaklands Hotel has been renamed
Sizzlers. The Cae Castell site has been flattened by the building of
houses. This is now Castle Avenue and Castle Crescent. The new
bricks shine. What is there left to see? Behind the bar no one knows.
As I exit to the car park I am followed by two entirely pissed women,
handbags whirling around them, clinging to each other's coats for
balance. This is Sunday afternoon. They've been out for lunch and
done two bottles and a half of Sizzlers' red each. It's here, slurs one,
gesticulating. Her arm waves in the general direction of a rubbish-
strewn slope. I climb through the fence and look out over the snaking
river and damp paddock below. Not a brick or carved stone block to
be seen. When Rumney Castle fell out of use as a defensive structure
in around 1270 it was turned into a manor house and home for

Gilbert de Clare's mother, the Countess Maud. Noble blood. You'd think something would be left to mark the fact. All I can see are weeds. The staggerers reach their battered Maxi, giggling, dropping their keys in the gravel. You shouldn't get into that, I tell them. I can see snow out there on the hills in the distance, way beyond the city. Why not, they shout. They both sprawl into the rear seat and leave the vehicle driverless. Better than going home.

Further up the hill are Rumney Hill Gardens, a small, well-manicured collection of tennis courts and bowling green reminiscent of a retired seaside town. Leading down into the river valley is a bridle path. Negotiating it is a bit of a stumble through woodland and bramble. But it's passable. It leads to a flat-bottom valley running north-east away from the city. It looks much like Cardiff must have millennia ago. Most of it. Green. Quiet. In the far distance I can see a rugby game and some low changing rooms. On the hillsides themselves are the great networks of orange brick estate – to the south immense Llanrumney and the north, above the Eastern Avenue road link, Llanedeyrn and Pentwyn. But the valley itself stays largely empty.

The path heads through reed beds for the river, and then follows it on out and far away from the diesel and grit of the stainless steel city. The silence comes in like a cloud. Water, soft sound of the Rumney. The places it passes now are nearly all pre-industrial – Church Farm, Bridge Farm, White Barn, Tai Derwen, Ty Hir Farm, Minorca, Gwern Leyshon Wood, Coed Craig Ruperra, Draethen. The river snakes and turns. The Welshness of the landscape re-asserts itself. The ground slowly swells. The past is back. I can feel it. But Cardiff – city and capital – that's gone.

ADAMSDOWN

I enter Adamsdown from the south by the Black Bridge across the rail line. Adamsdown took its name from Adam Kyngot, who in 1331 was a porter at Cardiff Castle and who farmed here. "A large piece of land – a messuage in the Parish of Roath" is what John Hobson Matthews calls the district in his Victorian *Cardiff Records*. A messuage is a piece of land on which a dwelling house is erected. They've certainly put up a few of those. Little sign of Kyngot now.

This is workers' housing, rail siding and drinking club territory. The Black Bridge is one of the oldest in the city, built in 1850, same time as the Broad Gauge rail line arrived here from Gloucester. It's a mess of black iron-girders and massive bolts filled in with bitumen-painted corrugated sheet. It's supposed to be pock-marked with German machine gun shells from 1943 but among the rust and rivets of time I've never found any. The bridge rises from the newly built but rarely open Sanquhar Street India Centre[16] to drop into Kames Street, Pertuce Ltd, *loans arranged*, green-shuttered, windows barred, the Adamsdown Gospel Hall and a sprawl of urban paint spray that goes back thirty years.

In the eighties a "working class" writers group established themselves here. They were true socialists in the spirit of Centreprise in London and viewed democratisation of the form as vital. Members would move out from their garrets to create a genuine writers co-operative. The politics of the group's actions were as important as their actual literary output. They set themselves tasks: write a paper on what you think we mean by 'working class culture'; discuss how established cultural institutions are one-way conveyor belts for ruling class ideology; why is the cultural struggle not a safe struggle? The group's activities were powered by alcohol rather than dope. They needed that engaging steam. A drug hazed floating mind usually leads to no more than beatific smiles.

In order to achieve their lumpen proletariat aim of disestablishing literature the group, dressed mainly in airware[17] and flighties[18], took over a section of the recently pedestrianised Queen Street in the city centre. They affixed to its surface the text of poems which proved their point. *Change the past. Do it now. We are Albion. We are Blake reborn.* They handed out the same texts mimeographed up as A5 flyers. They sat down. Completely ignorant of the country in which they operated, or possibly not caring, they acted as they thought writers might have done when the Winter Palace was stormed.

Strong. Supporters of the workers. Some of them were workers, of course, although most didn't bother. Resolute.

I watched all this from my city centre bookshop – I was running the Charles Street Oriel at the time and felt I'd already put in my time as an activist. I'd faced down the capitalists. Stood against the monoglots. Been out there street-selling verse. I'd read it loud to drinkers in pubs who didn't want to know. I'd stood on platforms declaiming. I'd handed it out as leaflets, free. There's only so much that outrage can accomplish. My stuff was now inside books that you could only unlock if you bothered to find them. Vision. History. Process. Art. Neat and clean. These streetwise literateurs were into dirty direct action, confrontation, opposition. They used poetry that went well beyond its constituent words.

The actual workers' reaction to the Adamsdown performance was, as might have been expected, mute. The local press ran a report about new romantics and how poetry was once again on target in its world game of moving itself closer to the people. If you listened to the media you'd imagine that poetry had been steadily doing this for the past fifty years. The people remained unmoved. Back in Adamsdown the writers drank from cans outside the Great Eastern[19]. It was summer. The light came in shafts through the plane trees, warmed the dust of the yet-to-be-traffic-calmed streets. Thatcher was at the helm and poll tax was looming. Poetry makes nothing happen, said Auden. Could he have been right? Soon Militant would galvanise the local population into a red wedge of disobedience. Can't Pay Won't Pay. Fight the Tax. No Poll Tax Here. The slogans would adorn the Black Bridge, the walls of pedestrian underpasses, and every green telecoms relay box from here to Canton. The battle had a vigour and engagement which their poetry somehow could not touch. Who wanted alien, distant Blake when a real battle like this was within grasp. The poets changed texts for diatribe and their pens for spray cans. The struggle continued. It always does.

Turning right just before the Great Eastern I track along back streets full of speed humps and front doors which open directly onto them. Adamsdown's Edwardian worker's housing might have been much better than Newtown's unsanitary back-to-backs but it still lacked space. Road grit lines the window edges. Old newspapers blow along the paving. At the back of Clifton Street, the frozen chicken warehouse has I LOVE YOUR MUM'S TITS scratched into the paint of its anonymous doors. This is one of the council's inner-city bike ways. Blue signs on poles. Marked pathways. No one on them but cars and dogs.

This is also Lloyd Robson territory. A post-Poll Tax scribbler with a neo-dadaist hatred of capital letters he has now made Cardiff poetry very much his own. "yu nose ow splott sounds bad ri? so we'r told any road, cos it' sounds liek SPOT or *SPLATT*!" Ask some of the swooney women after one of his stuttery performances at Chapter. Robson has eclipsed his rivals. Streetwise, football, dope, articulate. His *Cardiff Cut*, billed as a novel but more like a long poem, tells the whole tale and has earned him a real legitimacy. The heavy streets. The hard streets. The hooligan streets. Not those of the past but the ones alive right now. Robson has spent much of his time photographing the road signs and obtuse graffiti of here and nearby City Road. His montages are worth any amount of classic reportage. How we are in these tough places and the ways in which we change are his territory. Edge Territory[20]. Look him up. It's around 11.00 am as I cut through Diamond Street, along Cecil Street and on to Broadway. Robson doesn't do mornings. I don't knock his door.

THE LOCOMOTIVE

Broadway's The Locomotive, named after Stephenson's Rocket or Trevithick's Penydarren or Brunel's broad gauge or anything on wheels with steam and vitality and power, has been packed. Folk club. Upstairs, bare boards, fal da liddle, o me hearties, I'll go no more a rovin, hand on the brass belt buckle, finger in ear. The Hennesseys have been doing it at full strength, Irish Cardiff, pre-protest, folk as reinvented tradition, nothing yet in place to change the world. Between The Locomotive and the flat there are three further pubs and a working men's club with a doorman and a committee. We raggle taggle gypsy o along the pavements. 10.30 stop tap. These are the early sixties. Cardiff lags. Drink is a demon. The city fathers hold it back with a righteous hand.

By the two thousands the City centre is awash with bars which will serve you anything at anytime, thousand drinker capacity, standing, flavoured shot, lychee tequila, cocktail fish waste, liqueur lipstick,

single malt Red Bull, aniseed Guinness, glasses that dance, bend and melt. Life Bar, Fruita Bomba, Barfly, Liquid, Moloko, Gate Keeper, Edwards, Las Iguanas. Capacity has increased exponentially to house the hoards that reach here from the city's immense hinterland. Silver oblivion. Ice and glass. A sort of 2004 funfair for the alcoholically certain, blaring through the streets in their legs and naked arms. If Cardiff didn't provide for them then somewhere else would. If alcohol wasn't available then they'd use drugs instead.

A hundred and fifty years earlier Broadway barely existed. The Royal Oak stood at the end of Green Lane. Pub for scattered villagers. No Locomotive. No New Dock Tavern. No Clifton. The road to Newport was being developed as a residential district for merchants and fine families. By the mid-twentieth most of those mansions had fallen to investment landlords who installed multiple bell-pushes and yales on internal doors. I got here in 1966. Phil Ochs I Ain't Marching Anymore. John Mayall live at Klooks Kleek. Alexis Korner at the Marquee with the legendary Cyril Davies on harmonica. Blowing a storm. On brand new Radio One the Rolling Stones talked about listening to rare records shipped in from the Mississippi Delta. Crippled Hard-Armed Davies. Broke-Down Frank. Pannier-Tank Thomas. Blind Boy Probert. Harmonicas blew like blue saxophones in bedsits across the land.

The Hennesseys and their followers filled the flat's middle room. No space to sit. Stand and chant. Drink and wail. The docker down the hall, up at 5.00 am, threatened me with a heavy duty wrench. Slapped it up and down in his hand. Shut the crap up. I showed him my key of G Horner Marine Band. He took it. Bit it like a carrot. Bent the sides together. Handed it back. Here you go, sonny boy, try blowing on that.

I wrote blues lyrics. Didn't know you had to sing them. Broke down engine. Driving wheel. South bound train. Big fat mama. Been and gone. Gave a sheaf of them to Willie Dixon encountered outside the Colston Hall, Bristol, after a visit from the Rhythm and Blues show. Can you sing these? The big black guy in the broad rimmed hat, bass on at least half of Chicago's post-war electric blues, stuffed them into his deep inside pocket. Thank you, man, I'll read them when I get home. I really believed in these things. Finch at Chess Records. South Wales blues invade the delta. Just as damp there as here. I waited a while. Heard nothing. Career over. Blues done gone.

For a brief time I hung on as the district's Little Walter, Vamper in C, wailing. Walter used larger mouth harps, chromatic 16 hole. I could never get that tenor sax-like soaring. Wrong instrument, hopeless technique. I owned a set of five: couple of key of C, one E, one D, new G to replace the one the docker ate. Shining in their boxes, screws you could loosen, notes you could shake. Super Vampers. They were the only kind. Never found a plain Vamper on sale anywhere. Proud. What did folk singers know about harmonica music? Blues was deep. When the crowd left after the Hennesseys had finished so did my instruments. Lifted by some no-hoper needing cash. Took the pouch I'd made to hold them. And the electric pick-up. Resold. All I was left with was a penny whistle and a cracked ocarina. What kind of future was that?

Folk moved on from the Locomotive. Fashions changed. Back room of the Oak became a band room. Red Beans and Rice. Electric. Post-blues. Locomotive went sport and family. Its like that today. Benches on the roadside. Eighties plus. In a web survey the pub scored an average 7 for *Likelihood Of Leaving With Your Bones Intact*. The HB is decent enough.

THE ROAD TO CARDIFF GATE

The Cardiff Peripherique is a lane. In the north east, near Cardiff Gate, it isn't wide enough to let two Mercedes pass. It's thick with people carriers and fast Audis loaded with shopping. St Mellons Road, resurfaced, a suburban ring. This is the far reach of Cardiff's vast easterly housing expansion which runs from Cyncoed to Cefn Mably. 18,000 people swelling the City fast towards three hundred and fifty thousand. You can hear the lads playing soccer in the fields below, three games with nets and corner flags running simultaneously. The land here was once poor farm and slowly rising wood. This is Llanedeyrn then Pentwyn then Pontprennau. Cardiff's perfect mass housing. After the high rise debacle of the sixties we got it right this time. Almost.

I'm outside Cardiff Gate B&Q, the biggest store in Wales, watching the zoo. People who never go out anywhere emerge carrying sinks, fence panels, rolls of floor covering, huge ceramic pots. The thinnest girls this side of California with jewelled mid-riffs and studs above their lips smoke with professional intensity. A giant of a man with a belly that would flatten most counters it came up against drinks from a family-sized bucket of coke, three straws, slivered ice, fries, double whoppa in his other hand. Two pensioners emerge bearing strip-pots of alyssum, lobelia and marigold. There's a woman in Yobbie Slip Nike trainers and Miu Miu handbag. She wears full eastern black jilbab with contrasting light-grey niqaab face-cover up to her eyes. She manoeuvres a bundle of planed wood into a waiting Porsche. It's like the Klan are back. The required-under-planning-consent bike stand, which leans at 45°, has space for two cycles. But this is out of town retail. Soft-furnishing, supermarket, petrol, car wash, Ibis, Holiday Inn, Burger King. The stand is empty.

Llanedeyrn, Cardiff's first bulge north-east of Cyncoed, was begun in the late sixties. The last gasp of council housing before Thatcher outlawed it. It's built on the Radburn[21] principle. Housing set around cul-de-sacs. Service roads at the back where the kitchens and bathrooms lie. Through roads circle but do not intrude. There's grass and space and light. Underpasses and bridges. Car and people separate. You can walk from home to park to community centre without ever encountering a boy racer. Unalloyed joy. Most of the early-phase build were close terraces, stepped up the slowly sloping

hillsides. They were marketed as link housing to a generation who had never known the two-up two-down palaces of their forefathers. Terrace was a dirty word.

Pentwyn – the name the Council have now adopted for the whole district – is Llanedeyrn's extension. It is built on land north east across the Nant Glandulas, the trickling tributary of the Rumney which originates on the Caerphilly ridge. Rather than culvet, the stream is the feature of the small park that's been built around it. When I arrive the Environment Agency Community Fisheries promotion is in full swing. The small lake is surrounded by middle-aged, smoking anglers. Some watched by their wives. Nobody reading a paper. Burgers are being cooked. Local kids are amusing themselves at a sponsored coconut shy. Past joys unexpectedly return. Beyond is the leisure centre, sweat, tattoos, women with their hair in pony-tails and bearing rackets.

Pentwyn is at least 70% owner-occupied, and far easier to live in than other Cardiff estates to the south and the west. The thin scattering of pubs all have betting shops to their rear but don't quite look like the fortresses I've observed elsewhere. The churches blend into the landscape as if they were afraid to stand out. The clusters of shops all have full-front steel shutters. There is scribble on the underpasses and scatterings of Castlemaine and crisp packets among the bushes. But on the whole it's green and easy. Few speed humps. Nobody roaring through on a Honda. Not while I was there. Pentwyn (*Pentwin*, as most Cardiffians pronounce it) – *the top of the tump or mound* – is one of the most common place-names in Wales. And you know that's where you are from the street names – Bryn Pinwydden, Clos Y Gelyn, Waun Fach, Llwyn Castan. Socialism locates people with their land and their history. Pennsylvania curving along the remnant of wood that still bears that name. Coed-y-Gores on the land of Coed-y-Gores farm.

Further north, almost imperceptibly, Pontprennau begins. Pontprennau – *bridge of the woods*. Nineties new build for owner occupiers, no social housing, a surreal Disney landscape of orange brick and instant garden. An art and crafts hipped roof has a thirties bay projecting from it, fake Elizabethan half timbering, mock Victorian doorway, block drive, open plan front lawn with palm trees. The street names are the give-away – The Farthings, Greenacre, Butterfield, Almond Drive, Nasturtium Way. Chosen by developers determined to make their investments work. The clay and mortar have barely been washed clean from the pavements and already the dog walkers and Range Rovers have taken over. Who'd buy Glyn Eiddew when Peppermint Drive was available? I asked someone in the street which district I was in and she told me Cardiff Gate. The new world a million miles from the old town wall. Pontprennau is an alien Welsh mouthful. Won't last.

GWENNYTH STREET

Upstairs at the John Tripp Award the poets are cranking it out. Someone's doing a soccer poem while simultaneously bouncing a football with his right foot. It doesn't land until the poem is done. Steve Andrews, the Bard of Ely, appears dressed in full warlock robes and with an illuminated model of a flying saucer on his head. Tom Morrow has on a gas mask and carries a didgeridoo. From outfield a Chris Ozzard clone recites while twirling a cassette player at high speed around his head. The player is running a recording of the poet reciting. The effect dopplers around the assembled poetry lovers here for the beer or the shouting or the fun. Tripp would have loved it. Would he? The Award is an annual affair part-financed from JT's small legacy and supported by the Academi. How many of the entrants have read the great man's work? Probably none.

JT was regarded by many as one of Wales' best performing poets. And this from an era well before that term had come to mean anything at all. JT could do it. Stand there, laconically drawing on a cigarette, command attention simply by appearing in front of a microphone. His verse, delivered slowly, emphatically, could move audiences. Others shuffled their papers, lost their places, forgot what time it was when they started. JT simply roared ahead. Master of timing, a man who knew what the stage was for. While more famous poets bored for fifty minutes, flattening their audiences into the backs of their chairs, JT pitched it low. Enough and that only. Leave the listeners wanting. Sell them books later on. He was famous, after all. He was Penguin Modern Poets No 27. Black backed, paperbacked. Him and Ormond and Emyr Humphreys up there with Ginsberg and Bukowski and Ferlinghetti.

John had read at most of the pubs in Cardiff where readings happened, as well as in a fair few where they did not. He'd done *Horse* at Chapter, *No Walls* at the Marchioness of Bute, poems and pints nights at the Moulders Arms, The Queen's Head, The Lifeboat, The Greyhound, The Blue Anchor, Glamorgan County Council Staff Club in Westgate Street, The Royal, The Park, The Angel, The Central, The Golden Cross, The Big Windsor. Anywhere, everywhere, right across the city. But never Whitchurch – he lived there. His style suited pubs. Noises off didn't matter. Drink at hand did. And a mellowed audience always seemed to enjoy themselves much more than sober blue-rinsed sitting-up-straight listeners managed. Tripp, alcoholic heckler and loud complainer at other people's readings, the man who began incensed and then went to sleep, never did this at his own. For personal appearances at Oriel, The Reardon Smith, the Students Union, Lears Bookshop, The National Museum, and at City Hall he was professional to the core.

One place John never visited, although he always said he would, was the Gower in Gwennyth Street. Next door was Ned Thomas's University of Wales Press. Eventual publisher of the collected definitive editions of Glyn Jones, Roland Mathias, and Harri Webb. The area had lit cred. The Gower was a large and rambling Brains emporium with countless bars, snugs, smoke rooms, skittle alley and rambling upstairs function suite. It was built in speculative Victorian days as a hotel for the hoards thought soon to be arriving by railway. But they didn't. At least, not out here in north Cathays. The pub did well as a suburban refuge for meetings of the anti-Nazi league, the Socialist Worker party, the local fishing society, the allotment holders union and, for one of the great formative periods in its existence, that enterprising platform for burgeoning performance poetry, Cabaret 246.

Cab came on stream more or less as JT was leaving it. John had grown a mature moustache and had taken to spending weekends lunching in country pubs with his partner, Jean Henderson. He was not against the new style of performance poetry, at least as far as I could tell, but somewhat indifferent to it. The form's glory days were to come, anyway. John's were past. He'd been a founder member of the Welsh Union of Writers, drinking and debating with everyone else at the inaugural meeting in Llanerch in the summer of 1982. He's in the centre of the group photo, sitting, flanked by Cliff James and John Osmond and with Chris Torrance over his left shoulder. I think he slept overnight on the floor. Quite a few Union members were now Cab supporters. It was the future. Stage poetry, verse with props, histrionic arm waving. So many thought.

In the autumn and winter of 1985 Cabaret 246 had done well. Turn out was high. Arguments frequent. Public performances regular. There was a buzz, a magazine and a stage. Cab's artistic purpose was to bridge the gap between voice and listener, making poetry performable anywhere and against any sort of backdrop or interruption. Poetry you shouted. Poetry you sang. Poetry you recited without a script. Learned by rote. Read off scruffy bits of paper you'd just yanked out of your back pocket. But the way of doing it was hardly revolutionary. Members sat around the room, listened and commented, much like writers circles of old. Anthony Howell, archdeacon of art performance but a pretty straight poet, was a central presence. So were Ifor Thomas, Tôpher Mills, Gill Brightmore, Jonathan Brook, John Harrison and the late and legendary Bob R.S.Thomas. Dafydd Wyllt, later imprisoned for sending post-9/11 white powder to Rhodri Morgan and Jan Morris as anthrax, came late and stood around at the back. JT never went. He died on 15th February. I'd just come back from London visiting Bob Cobbing to hear the news from Nigel Jenkins[22]. Heart attack, on the couch, after a few beers. 56 years old. Bloody hell.

The funeral, an agnostic affair, is on a freezing day at a packed Thornhill where Roland Mathias presides. As a lay preacher he manages to make the whole thing slightly Christian without actually being so. JT arrives at a slight angle, pall borne by the unevenly tall John Osmond, Ned Thomas, Duncan Bush, Robert Minhinnick, Cliff James and myself. Glyn Jones speaks. Nigel Jenkins reads a poem. We all sing Cwm Rhondda. Glad to do this together

We need to raise the money for the wake. John's last diary entry reads "Went to Usk with J. *Very cold.* Pissed". Jean suggests raffling John's last whiskey bottle. Paul Tripp, John's aged blacksmith father, says he'd prefer a whip round. This is what we do. Money is collected outside the crem. We get enough.

The Wake is held at the Gower – like Cabaret 246 but with a massive mainstream audience. The long upstairs room is packed to capacity with both the BBC and the WUW recording proceedings. Almost everyone who is anyone in the literary world is there. Dannie Abse, Tony Curtis, Ray Handy, Duncan Bush, Dai Smith, Robert Minhinnick, John Morgan, Robin Reeves, Sally Jones, Janet Dube, Glyn Jones, Alison Bielski, Meic Stephens, Ifor Thomas, Bob Thomas, John Morgan, Graham Jones, Dan O'Neill, Tony Goble, Chris O'Neill, Ned Thomas, Cary Archard, Mick Felton, Daniel Huws, Harri Pritchard Jones, Lyn Hughes, Jon Dressel and dozens more. And almost everyone reads too. John's poems, tributes, tales of past drunkenness and outrage, praise. Someone tells a joke he heard on television the night before and claims it to be the last thing JT ever said to him. Doesn't matter. We all laugh. The myth begins.

Towards the end of the show, at a time when the fragile have departed and most of those who remain are full of Dark, Y Côr Cochion Caerdydd (the Cardiff Red Choir) begin to sing. For me their radical left-wing stance seems slightly at odds with JT's more moderate socialism, but I let it pass. Others, however, do not. Already there is a ground swell of appropriately JT styled drunken muttering and, as the Choir move into a South

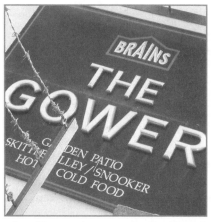

African freedom song with loads of wailing and open mouthed hwyl, a drinking friend of JT's from the Plough in Whitchurch begins to thrash about. Could it just be the beer? No. He shouts something about this being not what John would have wanted and lunges forward. In swift succession he hurls two glasses and a plate of sandwiches at the singing socialists and has to be restrained by Robert Minhinnick, quite a sight in itself. The Choir change quickly to *Hen Wlad Fy Nhadau* which drowns the disruption and gets the whole audience singing. Tripp's spirit roars about the room like something out of *Ghostbusters*. The choir finish and I read John's 'Notes On The Way To The Block' as a finale. It's done. The early muttering about the Union hijacking the funeral seeps into nothing-ness. Hijacking? It would have been just like this if he'd organised it himself. White bread sandwiches and battered crisps remain on the table. We leave. Us to bed and JT into orbit. He's still there.

He's got a memorial bench now and an award. But not yet a monster, definitive, *Collected Poems*. It would sell, wouldn't it?

East Cardiff

The white wall was much longer. The number of books in the study makes the beams creak. The gunera reaches for heaven.

The churchyard was a hill fort. Iron age ghosts inside
the circular walls. The river dried. The basement
of the Churchhouse still floods at high tide.

Dannie Abse in the gardens scratching his name. Rawlins White
pulling mackerel from his henges in the Rumney River.
Death by pestilence not heart attack. Water in the
land like blood.

Residents confuse riot with litter. Complain. The Gardens full
of polystyrene. Arm rest gone from the benches. Milestone
end of Four Elms Road rain wasted.

Shifts: Rath. Roarch. Rhuth. Raz. Reurch. Roarth. Reith.

The sea wall translated into MIME format.

Pengam full of burned out German planes. Orange
brick. Persimmon. Wimpy. Tucker. Goods yards.
Unweathered aspect covered with sunset fire.

On the site of the Roath Brick works, reen, tidefield,
clay bog. Raped and left half-naked. Welts.

Bird swarm. Redshanks. Dunlin.
The causeway east crosses two bridges. Evidence in the
mud of men smoking. Clay back to clay.

No one east of the pottery owned a piano. Songs sung
as the Roman road sank, stones gone for walls, passage
now untraceable: Hit The Road Jack; The Road I'm On;
On The Road Again; Take Me Home, Country Roads; Ride
That Tiger; The Long And Winding; Ride Me Ptolemy;
Maximus, Show Me How To Get Home.

The books weigh

We do not read them
We look at them
We shine their spines
The correct Roath had no women two Jews hardly any
history.

I take the books in a station wagon to the landfill and dump
them. Poems that tried hard. Hovered. Hung on for thirty years.
Staple rust. 64 mil pulp.

Roath limits: remember; found; list; told about; posted.
Loan words lead nowhere. There is nothing under the
soil in the garden bar clay and clay and finally shale.

The Ratostabius River (unknw)

Great house with its obtrusive, added columned porch. Yard
and stables converted to rooms where the dead get laid.
Grounds eroded by roads. Bus lane through the gatehouse
the smithy under strip development then flats.

Greyhound.

Love, desp
alley

Cymrectitude blind.

Coal was a bacillus staining. Dock
line in a ruck of trees. Gone.

Cinder foundation, I'm told. Black mortar. Red brick.

Key words: Colchester; Dorchester; Albany; Marlborough;
Waterloo; Sandringham; Kimberly; Blenheim; Harrismith; Alma.

Rain from the west, sheet and sheen. I dig down to look
for them, the cinders. Orange clay like a lifted body part. A kidney,
maybe.
A stomach lining. A liver.

Hole watches me, empty.

Winks.

Then fills with water.

LLANRUMNEY HALL

I'm driving up Rumney Hill. I'm slow. I'm legal. I go over the white-
painted speed camera markings at 28. There's a Mondeo pushing
hard behind me, driver yapping into his Nokia, cigarette, one hand on
the steering wheel. Overtakes. Nothing will happen. He's been in the

city, selling spoons to the restaurants or insurance to construction, and is now shit hot fast on his way to Newport to do it again. Speed snap. Doesn't matter. Someone else'll pay.

Beyond the Carpenter's Arms, where the hill eventually flattens and the grass begins, lies Llanrumney. Eastern Cardiff massif. Range on range of housing, black roadway, masonry path. I'm going there to look at the streets. Haven't done so for forty years. Northmore lived here. If I were Bob then he'd be Terry[23]. Ball Road. Bright new-brick council house. Glass front-door. Grass garden. Dad out of work. Retired or lost. Always there when I was, with his paper, his tea. Smoking. Radio doing worker's playtime[24]. When the toilet overflow dripped he didn't move. The council would send a man out to fix it.

Northmore was big on instrumental music[25]. Before the Beatles if you were not into Cliff Richard but still wanted to make your mark then that was mostly all there was[26]. You'd go into his tiny front room, squashed in between the three-piece (don't sit on it) and the glass-fronted china cabinet (empty) with the silver soda-siphon (broken) and fake cut-glass decanter (never been used), and there he'd be, Dansette record player, singles, guitar he'd built himself out of hardboard and fence paling. Wires running into the back of a giant 1930's valve radio. Screams and screeches. Feedback and roaring. Useless. Would be brilliant when The Who arrived five years later. But not now.

Out of the window you could see Ball Road's two black Ford Populars parked to save fuel. Trees. Football. And loads of light. Llanrumney was developed over a decade on the rolling eastern back

of the Rumney River as it snaked east and north. Green farmland. A few woods. Couple of cottages. Ancient Ball House, still there, estate built around it. Miles of sun and space. This was a post-war city expansion to house a rising population and to cope with the slum clearance displaced. Back-to-back crowding would become arm-stretch and breath. Disaffection would subside. People's lives would improve. We would love our concrete bus shelters, our community clinics, our phone boxes, our shops which sold Stork and Omo and Peter's Pies. The design was brick interleaved with air. Swathes of open grass would remain. Housing would nestle between trees. Views of the river valley and the Cardiff's rural northern slopes would be everywhere.

Northmore has gone now, of course. Moved on. Lost touch. I'm playing my Ventures Greatest Hits on the Sony CDX in his honour. *Walk Don't Run. Perfidia. Ram Bunk Shush. 2000 Pound Bee.* Driving on the long streets, traffic chokers, road humps. Past Fishpond Woods where kids on Suzukis and Hondas churn the sward into rugby-pitch brown. No litter. Not much broken. Parked Ford Fiestas. No feeling of threat. Two blokes in track-suits, identity bracelets, newspapers. A woman with a shopping bag. A Sunday single decker bus, mostly empty. A tyre in some bushes. A dog on a balcony.

Three-story Llanrumney Hall, at the bottom of Ball Road, looks like it shouldn't be there. A grade two listed Elizabethan mansion at the southern end of what the map calls the Lower Rookery. No rooks, few trees. The Hall ought to be surrounded by great gardens with an avenue running at its Doric-columned front door. Instead it has a gated iron fence, a car park full of white vans with roof-racks and ladders and a sign on a pole tastefully announcing POOL DARTS SKITTLE ALLEY – FUNCTIONS & PARTIES CATERED FOR. Pubmaster bought the mansion from the last owner, C C Williams, under a compulsory purchase deal at the time of Llanrumney's development in 1951. The historic significance of the Hall is immense. In Cardiff terms it is a great rarity – an extant building which has origins from well before 1600. You can count other examples on the fingers of a single hand. Originally a monastic grange belonging to Keynsham Abbey, the Hall passed to the great Morgan family in 1587. Born here were Edward Morgan, Deputy Governor of Jamaica and Henry Morgan, pirate and buccaneer There's a plaque commemorating the fact in the stairwell. There's a rumour, too, that the headless body of Llewelyn ap Gruffydd, Llewelyn the Great and the Last, killed at Builth Wells in 1282, was interred in a stone coffin which was set in the three-foot Hall walls. Discovered in the nineteenth century. Taken out. Celebrated. Re-interred. Gone now, or still there, or never was. Who knows for sure.

Outside the Hall is well kept. Painted stone cream. No double glazing. No neon. No inappropriate extension. Original Gothick windows. Even Llanrumney RFC's changing rooms, in an outbuilding round the back, are finished in keeping. But inside things have slid. The Hall opens into a large L-shaped bar with pool table, men in check shirts smoking, holding pints, eating crisps, and talking on their mobiles. The '50s conversion to pub remains more or less as it was when Northmore went past here playing air guitar, Cruel Sea by the Dakotas running through his head. Panelling. Heavy wood covered with scuffs and dust. The Morgan Room locked with evidence of buggering at the keyhole. Chairs and tables thumped a little. Lots of space. Wedding receptions catered for. Two resident beers. No sandwiches. Disco lights.

The Morgan coat of arms in mosaic sits in the surrounds of a great fireplace. They look more latter-day than original. The smoke-stained sixteenth century ceiling has lozenges, hexagons, fleur-de-lys, Tudor Roses, crumble and fleck. The music is Beyoncé then Dido. A bloke with an earring asks how I'm doing. Visitors here stand out like Martians. It would be good if I could find some Surfaris or Shadows or even Duane Eddy on the juke but among its 800 songs there are no ancient twangy instrumentals. We get Elvis. That's old. Sure is.

LLANEDEYRN VILLAGE

Where does the present take the past and completely annihilate it? Make it a shower of dust. Grey and valueless. Blow it away. Sainburys built on the site of the Roath Brickworks. Capital Tower erected on top of Greyfriars in central Cardiff. Whitchurch Castle flattened, now a car park north of Whitchurch High school on Manor Way. But there's a better place – the village of Llanedeyrn. Ancient. East Cardiff. Founded in the fifth century by St Ederyn, travelling west along the Via Julia Maritima. St Ederyn, hermit of Armorica, in the lineage of Arthur, in the bloodline of the holy grail, protected by winged serpents, by rods, by staffs, by swords. His place, vanished into the rapacious maw of new-build Cardiff.

The village of Llanedeyrn sits above a bend in the Rumney. Church, tavern, a cluster of cottages, farms, slow rising hills. Today it is flat-packed between the artics on Eastern Avenue and the fast cars

on the North Pentwyn Link. The route to the river is broken by an acoustic backwash. The sound of diesel rising through the trees. St Ederyn's sixth century Church towers white from among its rural headstones. Family tending a grave. Dog scampering. Yew hiding the porch. Organ rising inside. The puffy sleeves of the parson glimpsed through a crack as he performs a christening. The scene is shielded from the roaring by the thinnest line of lime and ash. Sun hits the dial high on the tower wall. Traffic makes it shake. Church House has gone. Church Farm is no longer agriculture. It's B.J. Skip Hire, high fence, gated yard. Protected by Camrasonic. Church Road which once ran all the way back to Cyncoed now goes nowhere, truncated in a bulbous mess of dumped freezers, wrecked laundromat fittings and hard core.

The Unicorn, established 1795, once thatched and with an oak settle and fitches of bacon under the beams, now trades as an olde-worlde out of town social experience. Quiz night, Sunday lunch, curry, spuds & toasties. The chalk board on the bar advertises pensioner's specials. A brass plate attached to an ancient pillar announces that "Floggings will continue until moral improves". Two lunch-time recalcitrants on high stools are in heated discussion about car gear ratios. The wire-fenced beer garden (rust, no plantings) feels like an east European leisure facility. In it the crowd from the christening are downing vodka shots and Heineken. Everyone smokes.

Boy-racers arrive on the road which goes nowhere via the entrance track from Pentwyn. They execute hand-brake turns below the church and then roar back out to terrorise the gardeners and dog walkers of Old St Mellons. *Old* St Mellons. The ancient parishes rename themselves in face of onslaught by housing. Llanedeyrn has given up. You only come here if you need god or a skip or a plate of steak and ale pie.

notes

1. Ptolemy, 87-150 AD, (also known as Claudius Ptolemaeus, Ptolomaeus, Klaudios Ptolemaios, and Ptolemeus) lived in Alexandria. His map making was speculative and drawn entirely from the observations of others. His world view was precise, delineating places and rivers and their relationship to each other through specific co-ordinates measured from a fixed, known point. His map of Albion and Hibernia looked rather like a snap of Britain stretched a bit by Photoshop and with Scotland turning sharp right at Hadrian's Wall. But considering he never actually travelled to the places he records his maps have an accuracy that is uncanny.

2. The Portway (the Julian Maritime Way) certainly went east from Cardiff but there remains argument about precisely where. Some historians place it along the line of the present Newport Road, the B4487 which runs along the ridge through Rumney, St Mellons and Castleton. Others suggest that it ran slightly further north, from Llwyn-y-Grant on out past Morgan's Tearooms, old Llanedeyrn village and beyond.

3. The thing with Twist and Shout was that you liked it and you hated it simultaneously. Liked it because it was loud and rough and easy. And hated it for the same reasons. It was an EP with its own picture cover and cost almost twice that of a single. Despite the price it stayed high in the charts for years. Only the Beatles could do that. Shake it, shake it. John Lennon rasping. You couldn't go to the concerts for all the screaming. What was the point when it was impossible to hear a thing? I had it explained to me following their 1964 show at the Cardiff Capitol "It's his legs, the way he moves them." Ah, sex. Should have known.

4. The Greyhound, Hayes-end of Bridge Street, last bastion of the poor of purse. The front bar had two pumps, beer and scrumpy. Scrumpy was a shilling a pint. In the back bar you could get scrumpy with blackcurrant added. That cost one and three. In the gents someone had written most of Allen Ginsberg's poem 'Howl' onto the tiles. New York reaches south Wales. Sort of.

5. Erected in 1966 in memory of Albert Norfolk Thorpe (1890-1963)

6. The village green would have been where the large Albany Road, Marlborough Road, and Waterloo Hill roundabout now stands. In summer I've seen people picnic here, sandwich and vacuum flask tea, the cars roaring round them.

7. Fully recovered, Flash now leads a quiet life with his owners in Kimberly Road.

8 Jeroen Van Westen, Netherlander, explorer of osmosis, photographer, builder, restructurer and regenerator of public space, artist.

9. Leachate is produced when water filters downward through a landfill, picking up dissolved materials from the decomposing wastes. Depending on the characteristics of the landfill and the wastes it contains, the leachate may be relatively harmless or extremely toxic. Generally leachate has a high biochemical oxygen demand (BOD) and high concentrations of organic carbon, nitrogen, chloride, iron, manganese, and phenols. Many other chemicals may be present, including pesticides, solvents, and heavy metals.

10. Rumney Park, in English. The name was chosen by local residents.

11. Name for the newly dug reen, again chosen by local residents. Local authority public consultation reaches a high level here.

12. The distance between the baseline of a line of type and the tops of the main body of lower case letters.

13. Dafydd Elis Thomas, Presiding Officer to the National Assembly for Wales.

14. For more on the poem and the site visit http://www.breathing-in.org.

15. The Eleventh Century Norman Lord of Glamorgan.

16. The Hindu Cultural Association Wales – www.hcawales.co.uk.

17. Doc Martens Airwair boots and shoes.

18. Green nylon US-style flight jackets: snap-close pockets (2 outside, 2 inside), knit cuffs, collar and waistband, and zippered combination utility/pen pocket on left sleeve. Skinhead jacket of choice.
19. Built on the site of Upper Splott Farm.
20. *Edge Territory* – Lloyd Robson's first poetry collection. Black Hat Press, 1995.
21. Radburn is a new-build satellite town of New York. Its name has been adopted as the generic name for a variety of late twentieth century housing estate development. Radburn's original planner was Clarence Stein.
22. Nigel Jenkins' fuller account of the death of John Tripp – 'It Was What He Would Have Wanted: John Tripp's Finale' appears in *Footsore On The Frontier, Selected Essays and Articles*, Gomer 2001.
23. Bob Ferris & Terry Collier. *The Likely Lads*. 60s BBC TV.
24. *Worker's Playtime* (1942-1964) – one of the longest running radio shows in history. A programme of music and comedy broadcast on the Home Service daily from a factory "somewhere in Britain".
25. Fentones, Packabeats, Blackjacks, Scorpions, Staccatos, Gladiators, Nu Notes, Cougars, Cannons, Federals, Outlaws, Tornados, Eagles, Saints, Consuls, Flee-Rekkers, Hunters, Wailers. Electricity. Amplified guitar. Music by white boys who could hardly play. The future.
26. Music historians often cite American instrumental rock and roll of the fifties as the forms precursor. Bill Justis, Cozy Cole, Bill Doggett, Johnny and the Hurricanes, Duane Eddy, Bill Black's Combo, the Champs. But these were mostly saxophone-led, teenage outgrowths of rhythm and blues dance music. The British form centred on the electric guitar and, ignoring brilliant American rocker, Link Wray, and surf music's king, Dick Dale, made the form Albion's own.

CENTRAL

ST MARY STREET

The lights are on. I'm entering the street of Saint Mary from the north. I've come out of Wharton Street squashed between Howells[1] – Cardiff's Harrods – and big Waterstones where poetry and Wales seem to have turned to dust. I'm just south of where the Street actually starts at Guildhall Place. The Town Hall in its stone-vase topped 4th incarnation was here until 1905 when they turned the town into a city and built a splendid new City Hall in Cathays Park. Before that, as the Gild Hall[2], it stood on medieval foundations in the centre of High Street. Roadways went either side of it. They were full of cattle, carts, tramped refuse and mud. Today it's Christmas and the street feels much the same. Fairy lights on the lamp posts. Revellers in half dress. Bare midriffs, skin shoulders, bow ties, glitz and glitter. On match days the police cordon off the street to traffic and the roadway fills with rugby's pissed and surging thousands. It's like that now. 7.00 pm. Dry. A slow moving line of mixed traffic strung about with roaring drunks. Ibiza uncovered in the south Wales gloom.

St Mary's – the church after which the street is named – vanished as long ago as the seventeenth century when the ever snaking Taff once again repositioned itself. It washed away to sea the remainder of the town's west walls, the St Mary's graveyard, the Great Close and all its tenements and then St Mary's itself. Some corbels, said to have been saved from the river-wracked church fabric, are reputed to be incorporated into the outer walls of Bute's replacement place of worship – the twin-towered St Mary and St Stephen's in Bute Street. I've looked and crawled but I can't find them.

It's hard now to trace the precise site of the original square-towered church. The river has once more shifted, been let into Brunel's new cut, and the land revealed – the Arms Park – enormously built upon. There's a church outline shown on the walls of the back of Wetherspoons Prince of Wales in Great Western Lane[3]. But this precise site is speculation. St Mary's, its graveyard, chapter house, tithe-barn, frater, dorter, preaching cross, burgage, chantry, hermitage, vicarage, stables, outbuildings, fishing hut and trout pond stretched up through the land currently occupied by O'Neills, Edwards Bar and the ground-floor swilleries of the Royal Hotel. The air of spiritual fulfilment stays with us still.

As I move south the sense of moral abandonment increases.

Dinner-suited youths piss in doorways. A bare-chested shave-head sprawls across the bonnet of a parked Mondeo. A middle-aged white-collar wearing a single earring and his shirt half out of his trousers falls off a traffic island. A girl in a short, sequined dress lies slumped again the window of a sandwich shop. On the back of a road sign is affixed the following notice:

> BE DISOBEDIENT – part of a global day of action in solidarity with the Argentinean rebellion. There will be a day of fun, disobedience and truly direct action against corporate bullying and greedy multi-nationals. Dress as Santa. Stop the traffic. Reclaim the streets. Make subversive success. Meet by the Nye Bevan statue, Queen Street. 21st December.

That's tomorrow. Someone comes up out of the Golate and is copiously sick into the doorway of the Bang & Olufsen showroom. No need. We are disobedient now. In our days of fun. We don't have to reclaim the streets. They've always been ours.

Crossing the junction with Wood Street, where buses bend towards the station and the edge of Riverside hoves into view, is like reaching the frontier. Surging hoards spin around the entrances to Wetherspoons. Black-coated, ear-phone encrusted bouncers watch from their doorways, overwhelmed. Fast-food boxes from McDonalds mix with cans and broken glass in the gutters. Someone comes out of the bowels of The Square, blinking, face full of blood, jacket smeared and ripped. A rubble of glass litters the floor of the Philharmonic. A line of shrieking girls with lace and lycra and breasts that pop bear WKD with them as they stagger among the stuttering traffic. Coffee Republic has its shutters up. A fifty-year old with the velvet-collared fawn coat of a lawyer or wide boy lies on the pavement outside La Brasserie. Arriving diners, tanked, middle-aged, loud, cigar smoking, ignore him. Women of a certain age with flashing-Santa earrings and decoration tinsel wound into their hair wahoo in a conga line. Their chubby knees and fleshy shoulders shake in rhythm. An overweight on heels with five plastic carriers full of presents, a French loaf and a box of Sainsbury's crackers leans against the end of the bus shelter, a full large glass of house red in one hand, king size in the other. Music roars out of Walkabout. They are dealing again, back of the Philharmonic. Guns and roses. But it's Christmas. They won't go off. The world is going to end soon. We are all going to be there when it happens.

St Mary Street has always been wild. O'Rourke's 1849 plan shows most of the southern end to be full of Taverns. The Ship & Pilot Boat Inn, The Royal Oak Inn, The Blue Anchor, The Cornish Mount Inn, The Pine Apple Inn, The Rock and Fountain. Nineteenth century pubs changed their names and moved site as much as they do now. The Blue Anchor located itself first near Cardiff Market, lost its licence in 1790 when the town's aldermen were going through one of their periodic fits moral guardianship[4], re-opened later next to the Terminus (now Sam's Bar) and finally came to rest on the site[5] of the old Ship and Pilot next to Gamlin's Music Centre. The career of this Hancocks two-ale bar with snug and back room resembled that of the Drifters, the singers of 'Up On The Roof' who still tour but no longer have a single original member. During its long life The Blue Anchor lost all contact with its original owners, licensees, clientele and location. By the twentieth century only the name remained: peripatetic, redolent of the sea, full of hope and oblivion.

In the late sixties Alan Bold, the Scottish poet, led a group of local hopefuls to the Anchor where a room had been rented for him to give a poetry reading. Bold was famous for presenting Harold Wilson with his slim volume, *The State of the Nation*, as a verse solution to the prime minister's monetary problems (Britain had de-valued its currency in 1967). Bold was an enemy of concrete poetry, abstract painting and dodecaphonic music. The avant garde was not for him. His new collection, *A Pint of Bitter*, was aimed at the masses and not the intellectual elite. Taverns were better places for its display than bookshops, of this Bold was certain. When we got there the pub was found to be both closed and in panic. Its basement had been flooded. South Cardiff, the familiar bog-land, was still subject to the whims of tide-borne water. Look at this, said the Landlord, showing me a set of wooden stairs that led down into swirling sewer-thick blackness. That's where the beer is. What are you going to do? Well, I'm not going down to get it.

Bold, who had no idea of Cardiff's geography whatsoever, turned out to be possessed of powerful survival instincts. With no guidance he led a straggling line of literature groupies, proto-poets and roll-up smoking hangers-on along Caroline Street with its wall-to-wall chippies, across Bridge Street and on up Union Street to the Moulders Arms. Here in the decrepit centre of the city, surrounded by walled up tenements, cobbles, broken roofs, brick-rubble and blocked gutters still stood one of Cardiff's oldest. If Cardiff had a Beat Hotel then this was it. The back room was a haunt of dope smokers, painters, jazz musicians and counter-culture insurrectionists. Bold's antennae were perfect. Can I do a reading in the bar? Cost you five pound. Done. Lost souls watched through Woodbine smoke. An unshaven checking the horses in his Daily Sketch paused. We bought halves and pints and peanuts and occupied all the heavy round tables. Bold did his bearded best, his Edinburgh accent cranked-up several notches for the occasion. He read about socialism, Scotland, the struggle, and the clear blue sky. Yu all enjoy tha? There was applause. No one had understood much but, what the hell, this man was big, as he kept telling us. Who wanted to argue.

In Christmas St Mary Street, the new millennium drive for oblivion is succeeding. Kitty Flynn's on the corner of Caroline Street, an Irish re-branding of the old Cambrian, is a sea of screaming. Someone has put in the window of Sportsales and BT's new blue Broadband Internet Kiosk has had its aluminium vandal-resistant keyboard covered with regurgitated veg. The Square are advertising £1 off all cocktails and three pints of Fosters for the price of two and the entire of south Cardiff have taken advantage. I look into Le Monde, one of Benigno Martinez's three Franco-Spanish sawdust, fish and steak restaurants that line the east side of the street. The place is a bedlam of whirling waiters, pink-faced overcoats, tight black dresses and coloured shirts. I consider retreating to Dorothy's Fish Bar in Caroline Street, last resort for all failed diners, but remember the rolling panic occurring on the pavement outside the former Cambrian. Give up. St Mary, tell me about Christmas. A passing gaggle of gregarious, tinsel-bedecked data typists give me a handful of party-poppers along with a number of invitations which I don't really fancy following up. There's a star-burst rocket gone off above the old Canal basin. Someone goes past on a bike with a four-foot Christmas tree strapped to the back. To the west there are stars. "It's so quiet now" wrote Alan Bold. Not any more.

CARDIFF QUEEN STREET STATION

On the Two-set up from the Bay a Malaysian student stands puzzled in front of Matthew Francis's poem[6]. "Wide wet walks where winds worry, weedgrown web-woven wilderness, wormy warrens, whiffling waters …" It's set in a frame like an advert for a day out at Barry Island or a visit to Caerphilly Castle. I can see her mouth moving in the shape of the words – "widdershins with whippy willows, wittering with whirligig wings". In her Bahasa Malay-English dictionary *widdershins* are not listed. We reach Queen Street and the doors open. Please stand behind the blue line marked on the platform edge until the train has come to a stand. That's one sign and there's more: Rizla Cigarette Papers – Smoking Can Damage Your Heath. Passing trains can cause air turbulence. Coke and Any Cake Same Price. Grappleable English. She seems relieved. We alight.

Cardiff Queen Street Station is at the eastern end of the city centre and is hemmed by the high rise of Axa Insurance, the Big Sleep Hotel, Ibis, British Gas, Landmark Place – "City Living Re-Invented", The Aspect Apartments, Brunel House. Viewed from a distance this is Cardiff new-age metropolis. Close up it's weather stain, buddleia and unfinished building site. On the map the station connects the Rhymney and Taff valleys with the city, the bay and the world. Rhymney, Bargoed, Llanbradach, Merthyr, Pontypridd, Aberdare, Treherbert, Treorchy, Penrhiwceiber, Mountain Ash. But trains no longer actually run to Maerdy, Penrhys, Rhigos, Hirwaun, Tredegar and other romantic memories of the industrial revolution.

The tracks there are gone. Lifted. Melted. You go by bus.

Queen Street itself was once a raggy suburb, outside the town walls. Full of beggars, street peddlers and women who made a slow living selling pots and crocks of veg. The suburb was Crockerton. Where the first Cardiff Infirmary once stood. Where the Theatre Royal played to the town's burgeoning hoards. Where the drunks rolled in the

mud and dung of the roadway.
Where the trams once ran, and
the trolley buses and the black
cars with running boards, the
Sunbeam Talbots and Ford
Anglias and Hillman Minxs
and Humbers. Where gas had
lit the highway since 1821.
Where the Leper Hospital of St
Mary Magdalene once had its
twenty-four beds and its faith
in God. Crockerton. Highway.
East of the East gate. Running

right to Ash Cottage, near present day Windsor Place. In 1850 the
easternmost extent of Cardiff. The Council renamed the highway as
Park Street in 1853. Then as Queen Street in 1886. Crockerton
residents declared it would remain Crockerton until the day they died.
Gone now. All that's left of Crockherbtown Lane, backing the stores,
full of dumpsters and delivery trucks. Runs from Park Place to
Greyfriars Road. Dark at night.

In its days of triumph, from Victoria to the death of George, the
Station built at the end of all this activity was a cathedral. Wrought
iron posts, glass roof, myriad platforms full of rolling steam, liveried
porters with two-wheeled trolleys, cloakrooms, uniformed atten-
dants, mail in canvas bags, signals with arms that lifted and fell.
Constructed originally of wood in 1840 as Crockerton Station the
rail terminus has a history of redevelopment. In 1887 it was enlarged
and re-branded as Cardiff Queen Street. This was Taff Vale Railway
enterprise. Goods yards and massed sidings lay beyond across the
land now occupied by Brunel House. Cardiff was a place where
money was made and the railway was its agent.

The Rhymney Railway, a rival operation, reached Cardiff through
the Caerphilly Mountain tunnel. Its first station was at Adam Street,
near Cardiff prison but as passenger operations grew a finer terminal
was established at the end of The Parade. Cardiff (Rhymney) station
opened in 1871 and worked until traffic was diverted to Queen Street
in 1926. The site is now occupied by an extension to the Physics and
Astronomy department of the University. Ground dug again, traces
lost. Not a mark anywhere on the new brick and tarmac surface. From

the lecture rooms students watch the two-cars rattle. Gaudy Valley Lines, full of colour and urban flash. At the end of The Walk, which parallels The Parade there's a cast-iron fence post with an angular section that reeks of Victorian railway. All that's left of the Rhymney and its great adventure. Its mineral wealth could have gone to Newport and changed that city's fortunes. But it came here. Cardiff, iron metropolis, coal capital of the world.

The present Queen Street is a shadow of its former self. Its tracks reduced to three and its canopy to a late sixties pre-fab which lacks both style and glory. Only the over long platforms tell you that this isn't just another suburban halt. The Trans-Europe Express could arrive and there'd be room for everyone to get off. Magyars in long coats, Russians with fur hats, peasant women with brown-paper packages, Turks with moustaches and imitation-leather brief-cases. It could come, but it doesn't. Denis Morgan, the Station Manager, has been with the railway seven years and can't remember anything other than Valley trains. Three-hundred trains a day come through here, he tells me. Traffic is increasing. We are trying to re-open platform one. He points across the rails to the rough remains of the earlier enterprise, now cleared of weed, moss and mortar rubble. Why do they come to Cardiff? Drinking, shopping, Millennium Stadium, work. Where? See that building there? He points at the mirror windowed high rise next to Landmark Place on Churchill Way. That's the British Gas call centre. They work there. Wales like India. A thousand staff filtering calls from the entire UK. Bright, responsive. Letting their accents rip. We walk the platforms looking for traces of the past. A

couple of long wooden benches with the letters GWR set into their wrought-iron legs. Half a brick arch visible above the track on platform three. Some tiles near the stairs. Is it all gone? Only the old subway is left, locked, abandoned, running out under the Aspect Apartment's car park. Dark, uneven flags, dripping water.

The two-car trains bang in and out of the station at a

prodigious rate. Some of them have names – Tom Jones, University of Glamorgan – but most are just numbers. 142 sets. 143 four cars. There's a policy to name the trains now. It helps community relations. A green and red set from Aberdare arrives with a poem, *The Fall*, visible in its frame behind the drivers cab. Do you think we might get a diesel set named after Tony Curtis, I

ask? He wrote that poem. But I don't think Denis is listening. He's telling me something else. We get anorakers, he says, choosing the word with care. Blokes who take down the numbers. They like it best when we run Millennium specials. Real trains with engines and carriages with slam doors. And you should see the crowds those days. We've got to get the boys down in the street outside just to control them. Cardiff, irresistible. Queen Street Station is one of its portals.

Outside I cross Station Terrace, walk past Index, once the Alexandra Hotel, and enter Sainsbury's Metro on the corner of Dumfries Place. Through the store windows you can see the main line crossing Newport Road on a bridge which advertises Jeff Jones second hand Autos. We are well outside the old walled town here. Site of the Spital[7], Cardiff's medieval hospital. Its stream crossed through fruit and veg to exit through ready made salads in the direction of the feeder. Did you know they once treated lepers here, I say to the check out girl by way of conversation. She swipes my plastic-packed lo-cal chicken sandwiches and stares at me as if I had just arrived from Kazakhstan. Outside another 142 two-car beats its rattling way towards Merthyr.

SURROUNDING THE WELSH OFFICE WITH SALT

Cathays Park is still parkland – cherry, forsythia, azalea, tree mallow, alder, lime – you can walk here, lost in greenery. "Poets of the precincts – Lacking parallels – Instinct with the instincts – Should exchange Arcady – For the brick of Cardiff"[8]. But maybe not here. This is the Civic Centre. Between the trees are the white portland sides of the City's administrative capital.

This was all Bute's land until the end of the nineteenth century – an empty park across which he could exercise his horses; gardens through which he could saunter, smoking his cigars. The ground was enclosed from Park Place to North Road with a tree lined drive up its centre. This was the seventeenth century farmland of *Cate Hayes*. By the time Bute bought it its name had mutated to *Cathays*. The name is supposed to come from the Irish for the site of a battle (*cáth*) and the Norman French for a hedged enclosure (*haie*). Sound likely? I don't think so either.

Bute's burgeoning town had outgrown four town halls – usually because they had become too small, fallen down or caught fire – and the great Marquess was persuaded in 1898 to sell his 60-acre parkland to the Council as a site for the fifth. The space would be used to house courts, colleges, municipal offices and a museum. Bute set conditions. Avenues would bound a central park, buildings would be low, the air would stay clear.

The Baroque City hall with its believable dragon atop a St Paul's dome and instantly-memorable offset clock-tower was E.A.Rickards' winning design in a great architectural contest. There were fifty-six entries (contrast with the two hundred and sixty nine in the first competition for Cardiff's Millennium Opera House) and the new building was completed by 1904. It set the tone for the rest of the Park's development. The elegant white of the buildings' Portland visible through drifts of cherry blossom, wide red-surfaced avenues, statues of the founders dotted on plinths among acres of grass and herbaceous border. They all came here, the institutions – the Assize Court, the National Museum, the University Registry, Glamorgan County Hall, the Technical College, the University College, the great Temple of Peace and Health. And, until the escape of Cardiff Council to its pagoda at the bottom of East Dock, and the take-over of the Bay's Crickhowell House by the new National Assembly, this Park exuded ultimate power. A Welsh Washington. A graceful centre of the Welsh universe amid trees and grass. On the day that First Minister in-waiting, Ron Davies, issued his momentous decision that the National Assembly would not take over and refurbish the aging City Hall but would go instead to new premises in the Bay I found myself walking here. I was in the company of a newcomer to the City. They have to build the Assembly here, she said to me, this is the only place we've got in Wales that has the right authority. Sun on the grass. Old world grace around us. That was the problem, of course. Richard Rogers' glass debating chamber and steps down to the fresh-water harbour would face the way we were going. The twenty-first century. This peaceful place was redolent of the past.

At the top of Cathays Park, overlooking Alexandria Gardens and the war memorials, stands CP One, as it is colloquially known. This relatively undistinguished construction started out in 1938 as the headquarters of the Welsh Board of Health. It is more famous, however, for having spent most its twentieth century life as the Welsh Office. Centre for the administration of Wales by the governments of Westminster. Colonial HQ. Reviled and hated.

Behind it stands CP Two, CP One's tank-busting, fortress-like extension, built in the seventies. Triple-gated entrances, sheet screen, security comb, uniformed guards, barriers against attack by ram-raid and by bomb. Government occurs in the deep interior, bunkered and air filtered. Good morning. Guard in hat, no salute. Could I look around? No.

This place, now released into the wider world as more administrative offices for the National Assembly, was once the target of almost every popular protest organised in Wales. In their time the slow steps descending to College Road have been stacked with banners, placards, hay, cow dung, tractors, milk crates, car tyres, people, coal, cardboard, black-bagged rubbish, singers, dancers, men with loud-hailers, women with megaphones, face-painted children, animals, squatting pensioners, striking miners, irate residents, language activists, local bombers, students, the dispossessed, the out of work, poll tax rebels, drunkards, NHS wage-slaves, teachers, nursery nurses, fishermen, Christians, communists, creationists, crachach, peace women, peace youth, peace men. And the pissed off, loads and loads of them. They all go to Cardiff Bay now, where the winds are stronger. CP One stands lost and somehow vacant. Purpose down the pan.

While the building was still the detested Welsh Office the poet, Cymdeithas yr Iaith member and long-term surrealist, David Greenslade, surrounded it with salt. Greenslade, veteran of many a foray to America[9], had long been taken with the States' sixties history of linking arms around the Pentagon and surrounding the White House with flowers. The Americans once voted a pig to Congress. If Wales had a president to elect I'm sure Greenslade would have put up a pit pony. In 1996, completely hacked-off with 'official' support for the language, Greenslade decided to bury the centre of irksome officialdom in alchemically purifying salt. When he got to Safeway in Ely he realised that to completely cover the building he'd need rather more than they had on their shelves. Undefeated he opted instead for a surrounding. A continuous line burning pure and holy to contain the heaving demon. Safeway allowed him 56kg of cooking salt on sale or return. If you don't use it all, love, you can bring it back. Reassuring.

The day was sharp and frosty. The task took four hours and the salt cut a clean and healthy line into the icy ground. Using English a security guard asked Greenslade what he thought he was doing and got a perfectly polite reply, but in Welsh. I am pouring salt, said Greenslade. Dwi'n arllwys halen. The guard returned with an inter-preter and was told that the writer was acting in the interests of alchemical purity, yr hen iaith and the fate of Wales. Of course. The whole deal was recorded on video by poet Richard Gwyn and witnessed by Chairman of Cymdeithas yr Iaith, Gareth Kiff. A few office workers observed proceedings from their windows. When the line was complete Kiff, Gwyn and Greenslade went home. An article appeared in *Barn* and Greenslade issued a postcard of himself in mid-pour, photo taken by Reggie Tucker. Politics? Art? Way into the future? All three. "No salt, no experiencing – merely a running on and running through of events without psychic body" says Jungian psychologist James Hillman in the book *Salt and the Alchemical Soul*, a Greenslade favourite. Salt makes it all real. Try it yourself.

WOMANBY STREET

From where I sit I can see slate roofs, stone balustrade with sprout-ing buddleia, western sky beyond. Old Cardiff. Oldest there is. I'm at Undeb[10] in Womanby Street, the curving street of pirate battles, horse

manure, cattle market, clubs and pubs, distress and over-drinking that has gone on now for almost a thousand years. Womanby snakes its narrow way from the Castle to Westgate Street where the Taff once flowed and the Town Quay imported wine in exchange for cannon. Red light for decades but now improv-ing. Until recently Undeb was the CF1 Club, *Every Friday*
American Table Dancing At The Devil's Lounge. Now it's Sunday supplement modern. Slate floored lift. Chrome front door with inter-com. Owned by music biz operators, full of Welsh stars. I'm taking lunch with Grahame Davies[11]. The place is a new experience for both of us. Fine dining: pan-fried seabass with roasted scallops, herb-crusted lamb with a white bean and chorizo casserole, crab and basil mash with sauce vierge. You don't put your coat on the back of your chair, someone takes it from you. You get a waiter who brushes the crumbs from the tablecloth. The menu has slices, goujons, stacks, wedges, pendants, portions, medallions, dollops. There's music in the background but it stays there.

We're in the city, the real city, heart of the city, and it's new. Wales has no tradition of cities, of course. Until the nineteenth century the largest conurbation we had was Carmarthen with a population of over five thousand. Cardiff was far less. Twenty-fifth in the pecking order. In towns and villages you can know everyone. The alienation that wrecks bus shelters, bombs phone-booths and puts name tags on all available wall space is an industrial disease. A product of density. Something that happens because we don't know our neighbours, don't care, can't win, can't see anyway on or out. In Wales of the hill farm and the scattered community such pain hardly exists. Best we've managed, down the centuries, is a drunken brawl outside a market day tavern or a bit of thieving from a passing stranger or our richer masters. The Welsh, the underdogs. But the arrival of iron and coal and their attendant explosion in population ended all that.

In cities, where the great and the good mix with the lollard and the lumpen, proximity to the mass changes the way you think. Things are faster and there are more of them. You can no longer know everything because there is far to much of it. The thirty streets of your town become the three-thousand of your blossoming capital. Your village poet serving a few hundred houses becomes three hundred-and-fifty bards, novelists, dramatists, fictioneers, scribblers, hacks, journos and pad scratchers serving the surging mass of a recently arrived city hoard. Perspectives shift, culture and exposure to it increases, writing alters. Distance changes. The horizon is built on. The streets are lit. The night sky goes dark.

In the eighteenth century the scattered parishes of Y Rhath, Llysfaen, Rhymni, Treganna and Yr Eglwys Newydd[12] were monoglot Welsh. At least half of those living inside Cardiff town's crumbling walls were able in the language. But despite these origins a massive influx of outsiders has made the city today an overwhelmingly English-speaking place. How has it served its writers? Until recently not brilliantly well. Meic Stephens' 1980s *A Cardiff Anthology* collected the historical view of the city. Docks, smoke, coal, cockle markets, Arms Park, arcades, *Western Mail*, rap-tap-ginger in the slums. Some written by people not born here, not living here now, never lived here. Alexander Cordell, Jan Morris, Idris Davies, Alun Richards, Gwyn Thomas. More by those who didn't know each other, or didn't want to, separated by culture and language or by the stretch of the city's breadth. No sense of community. Literateurs operating in self-contained boxes. Mutual antipathy. Welsh writers divided from their Anglo fellows by miles of linguistic fence. My Cardiff not your Cardiff never ours.

Grahame, who is an outspoken satirist of the incongruities and follies of the Welsh-speaking media class to which he belongs tells me that he thinks Welsh-language writers in Cardiff have yet to develop what he calls "a comfortable urban discourse". The responses are disparate, there's no consensus yet. City life is still new. Walk down the street and hardly anyone recognises you. The rain here is so different from the rain in Flintshire. This is another world. Grahame should know. He's from Coedpoeth near Wrexham in Wales' north east, been in Cardiff for a mere seven years.

To paraphrase Adrian Mitchell, most writers, it seems, have ignored Cardiff because Cardiff ignores most writers. For the nineteenth and most of the twentieth century those writers there were either operated in total isolation (Dannie Abse's *Ash On A Young Man's Sleeve*[13], Bernard Picton's *Tiger Bay*[14]) or indulged in episodes of nostalgic ark ark the lark typified by Frank Hennessey and Pete Measey. Billy the Seal, Clarks Pies, Brains Dark. Tôpher Mills is their natural inheritor (although to be fair he has updated their line). Until the 1980s you could count the successful women writers from Cardiff on the fingers of one hand (Bernice Rubens, Gillian Clarke – both moved out because this city didn't suit them). No black writers either. Amazing for a place with the largest ethnic population of anywhere in Wales (8%).

In recent times things have improved, for the poets at least. Clustered around the Cabaret 246 performance group, Happy Demon, Pandora's Box, Sampler, Chris Torrance's Adventures In Creative Writing night classes, Seren's First Thursdays, or one of the many readings in the city's clubs, cafes and beer halls poets have always ensured that their voices can be heard. But are these genuine Cardiff voices? Not really. The poetry could be from anywhere.

I talk to John Williams about this in the Cottage, an old-style Brains pub on High Street. This is barely a stone's throw from Undeb but another world completely. Here the air is fog dense with tobacco, the 28-inch TV relays non-stop soccer and the locals look like they've just reached here from a lie down in the park. I've got a little digital recorder on the table between us but when I get it home all I can hear is the sound of goals roaring and the voice of the bloke at the table next to ours as he tries to get his roll-up alight, bloody thing, won't go. John is one of the leading lights of the late 1990s Cardiff fiction

boom. He reckons that the city feels more a south Wales Liverpool than the nation's capital. Cardiff is a place which mixes many nationalities with the Welsh being only one of that number, he tells me. The language, while appearing to be a left-wing cultural idea usually succeeds in alienating the largely monoglot English-speaking local working class who can't see the point of it. What relevance does it have to their lives? Instead, Welsh has become the would be lingua-franca of Cardiff's new media and governing elite. "Cardiff, once an overwhelmingly working-class city, is now becoming a city of haves in a land largely of have-nots. The further irony is that the most prosperous of the haves seem to be the incomers, the Welsh-speaking government and media types, while the monoglot speakers of Kairdiff English start to feel like second-class citizens in their own city.[15]" Despite this we have still managed a fiction push, and that's new. Des Barry, Sean Burke, Lloyd Robson, John Harrison, James Hawes, Anna Davis, and John Williams himself have all written about the city and have done so, often, in each other's company. Cardiff rather than Kairdiff or Caerdydd pulls this group together.

Grahame, as one might expect, sees things differently. Between spoons of broccoli and stilton soup he explains that in many ways Cymry Caerdydd share the experience of some Jewish communities, whose members are seen as being more prosperous than their gentile neighbours – literate, articulate and with ready access to the media. Or to vary the comparison, if blacks are a "visible minority" then the Welsh speakers are could be termed an "audible minority." Every time they speak Welsh to one another in public their difference is manifested. In such a position, any incongruous or unacceptable behaviour by a member of that community runs the risk of being used as a means of criticising that community as a whole. "You see one West Indian taking drugs and decide that they all take drugs. See one Welsh speaker with shades and a fast car and assume everyone else is the same. They are not. Most Welsh-speaking communities are poor." Is this in the literature yet? James Hawes touches on it in *White Powder, Green Light*[16] but the issue, a real one for Wales of the committees and the communities, has yet to be decently explored.

In terms of critical mass – that hard to pin down meeting of population density, cultural institution and contemporary acclaim – Cardiff has arrived. Much of its new fiction – *Cardiff Dead, Five Pubs, Two Bars and a Night Club* and *The Prince of Wales*[17] (John Williams), *Deadwater*[18] (Sean Burke), *Melting*[19] (Anna Davis), *Middleman*[20] (Bill James) – appears from London publishers. Cult works – Lloyd Robson's *Cardiff Cut*[21] and Leonora Brito's *Dat's Love*[22] have been published by local houses. Herbert Williams' *Punters*[23] has been a success for west Wales-based Gwasg Gomer. Trezza Azzopardi's retread of Bute Street through Maltese eyes, *The Hiding Place*[24], was Booker-shortlisted in 2000. The arrival of the National Assembly, even for its detractors, has given Wales as a nation the credibility it formerly lacked. Shirley Bassey, the one famous Cardiffian who loved us and left us, has even been seen wearing a dress made from the flag's red dragon. It's cool to be Cardiffian (even if the word cool itself is now suspect).

Whether this means that Cardiff is now a city state trying to rule the rest of Wales or a cultural epicentre with spokes that run to our far regional reaches is a matter for discussion. Our publishers are not here – they are in Bridgend and Cardigan and Llandysul. Our leading literary magazines are in Porthcawl and Aberystwyth. All is well and fair right across the literary world. But try saying that in the villages on Llyn, or in Pwllheli, or in Bethesda where everyone knows each other or in Llanystumdwy where they all drink in the same pub. Cardiff? It's in another country.

Cardiff Medicine

Moved the dispensary twice
because of demand.

Leeches, bloodletting, herb,
mineral, purge, laxative,
web of spiders, powdered nut shell,
wet excreta, dried cock windpipe –
to fix abortion, asthma, sterility,
cancer, dysmenorrhea, melancholia,
empyema, dropsy, worms.

The Spittal leaking water into Bute's
West Dock feeder

Fumitory, Borage, Bugloss.

Haze of dysentery in the brackish damp

Upset the roller rink by
building the infirmary on it.
The long cross lost.

You could die in this town

without pain. Manage it through
fear, god, alcohol, powder,
faith, talk, belief, let blood,
leak, white shining light, fog,
cross, miasma, chalice, belief,
brow, chant, shake, foam, rage, bite,
leech, hail, shout, cut, sweat, doubt,
doubt, & hate.

In 1967 when they excavated Greyfriars
to put up The Pearl twenty-six
stories full of light Llywelyn Bren dead
since 1315 returned in the digger bucket.
Below a heap of skeleton seen from
the shape of the pit as plague victims.
Medical panic put jean clad builders
into white atom suits so the infection would
not spread. Ah panic.
The Black Death back but it wasn't.

25 million people died in the years
between 1347 and 1352. Half the population
of Europe. There was repenting.
But the bubonic lymphs
still inflated.

26 hospitals in Cardiff 2002 (Google)

(unsubstantiated)

Source data:

Devil's Bit: Very effective for coughs, shortness of breath and all other diseases of the breast and lungs, ripening and digesting cold phlegm, and other tough humours, voiding them forth by coughing and spitting: it also ripens all sorts of inward ulcers and imposthumes, pleurisy also, if the decoction of the herb dry or green be made in wine, and drank for some time together. Four ounces of the clarified juice of Scabious taken in the morning fasting, with a dram of Mithridate or Benice treacle, frees the heart from any infection of pestilence, if after the taking of it, the party sweat two hours in bed, and this medicine be again and again repeated, if need require.

Spittal: East-West across centre of present day Newport Road. 1666. (Cardiff Survey). Schedule of the bounds and rents of the Lordship of Spittle. James Herbert esq. possessed the capital house called the Spittle, and 5a. of land, late in the tenure of William Bawdripp esq. deceased. Herbert Evans esq. held 8a. with 5 cottages & gardens, and the barn and orchard, all at Crockerbtown. Lands include site of present prison, re-pointed south wall, top armoured, all lead roofs, no slates or tiles. Two public houses adjacent – The Vulcan and Rumpoles – visible to inmates using mirrors on sticks. Incidence when I passed of female companion to inmate standing on top of road island traffic bollard holding up her skirt. Cheering from passing cab drivers and prison windows.

Bren: Ymysg rhestr o'r cyfnod o eiddo Llywelyn Bren ceir 3 llyfr Cymraeg, yn cynnwys copi o'r Cyfreithiau Cymreig, copi o'r gerdd Ffrangeg Roman de la Rose, a 4 llyfr arall. Roedd hyn yn gyfnod cyn dyfeisiad y wasg argraffu, ac yn tystio fod Llywelyn Bren yn ŵr diwylliedig, ond am iddo ymladd gormes, cafodd ei ladd gan draha y concwerwyr. His wooden tomb was still visible at Greyfriars when Rice Merrick passed in 1578.

dispensary moved to site of Great Heath racecourse
culverted Wedal River,
smoke stack on-site body part crematorium,
dental facility, A&E, Allah, fountain.
In Kibbor, Roath Dogfield, Roath Tewkesbury, Cardiff Friars, Roath Keynsham, Llystalybont, Llandaf, Splott, Spittal, Griffithsmoor, Canton, Plasturton, Whitchurch, Penarth, Cogan, Cosmeston, Llandough, Leckwith, Caerau, Beganston, Radyr, Pentyrch, Wentloog, Rompney, Mannocks Hold, and Wentloog Alias Keynsham – all early sites of places of cure – none.

THE TOWN WALLS

"I can understand you. It's these educated people that get in here. My posh customers. I don't know what they're on about at all." This is all spoken in gogledd Welsh. Heavily accented. It's like listening through fog. I'm in a taxi heading for the Castle. The driver is from Pwllheli. Long way from home. "What've you been doing?" he asks. "Walking the town walls," I tell him. "Didn't know we had any." "We don't." "Just like Pwllheli then." Except that Pwllheli didn't have any in the first place. Cardiff did.

According to the records the Normans built a wall around Cardiff after they invaded in 1091 and installed a keep on the battered remains of the old Roman fort. The wall was of wood, a palisade running along the top of an earth bank, a vallum. There was a ditch on the outer side. There were watch towers. Gates. A stockade to keep the Welsh out and the colonists safe. Wales was the wild west eight hundred years ahead of time.

Gradually wood was replaced by stone, which didn't burn. As medieval town walls went Cardiff's were typical. Gates were castellated. Watch towers strengthened. This didn't stop Owain Glyndwr who in the early fifteenth century knocked down whole sections and raised to the ground much of the town inside. It took medieval Cardiffians at least twenty-five years to recover. But by 1451 the town was back to full strength. New walls erected to repel all comers. Things were to last a hundred and fifty years, too, until the next attack. This one was not by the Welsh, but by the marauding sea. In 1607 the tide dramatically breached the Severn coast defences from the Usk to the Ely. Sea water reached Roath Church. Adam's down was water meadow. Canton a lake. You needed a coracle to cross St Mary Street. The walls were breached. Embankments subsided. Parts collapsed. Stones were washed away. Beginning of the end. And although rebuilding occurred things were never to be quite the same again.

I've been trying to track the size and shape of the old Town, the borough, by walking the route of its walls. This tiny place of Cardiff lords and burgesses, lost now in the heart of an enormous city. I'm doing the walk with Jonathan Adams, architect of the Wales Millennium Centre (WMC) and aficionado of old building stone and the way that roads once ran. As credential Jonathan can claim residence here during the 1980s. He had a flat in what he then imagined to be dangerous Roath. Pre-development Cardiff – city of skinheads and robbery, bustle and violence. It's not the same now. Brighter. Less threatening. But Jonathan is still unhappy. He sees

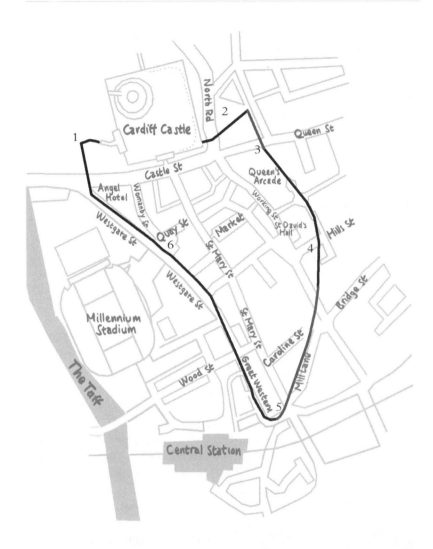

A MAP OF THE TOWN WALLS

1. The Westgate
2. Site of remaining section behind Bradford and Bingley
3. The Eastgate
4. Cock's Tower
5. The Southgate
6. Riverside Tower (outline of wall visible in carpark)

Cardiff as a city of missed opportunities. There's no strategy for long term change. Nothing in place to protect the best of what still exists. And so much damage already done.

As a guide I am using Speed's[25] 1610 map. There's no map earlier than this and Speed shows no wall along Cardiff's western side. History says that the Taff took it. Snaking on its flood plain, brushing the town, undermining the wall, taking the soil to sea. And then, when in flood, pulling the towering stones down. Until Brunel put it in the place it is now the Taff didn't stay still. Jonathan has a photocopy of the map Bute's estate surveyor John Wood made in 1828. We compare. The Taff is in different places on both of them. No sign of any western defences on either.

At their finest the Town walls were more than twenty feet high, ten thick, and with a parapet walk along the top. There were six gates, six gatehouses, with accommodation for the gatekeepers built in, and at least four watch towers from which to spot invaders and floods. Burgesses, merchants, and the well-to-do lived within them. The streets of old, old Cardiff were beaten mud and the houses were of timber. But the walls kept the enemy out.

There's plenty of speculation about where they ran too. Before Speed fixed them. Before the town grew towards the sea. Owen John Thomas reckons that the first wall went no further south than St John's Church, looping down from Kingsway to bend west towards the river where the Old Library is now. In his account St John's was for the Normans and vanished St Mary's for the native Welsh. Why was St Mary's built so far from the Castle? And why did a place as small as

Cardiff need two churches? Doesn't make sense. There's evidence to back his argument. Traces of ancient wall footings have been found in the foundations of Cardiff market and on the route to the river. But proof? Who knows.

Jonathan and I begin at the West gate, Burges' replica built onto the original foundations but with a new curtain wall added to link it to the fabric of the Castle. The road west from the town once ran through here. It went up through the Castle grounds to cross the Taff with a wooden bridge situated around 80 yards north of where the stone bridge is now. This was the Millgate[26]. The Miskin Gate[27]. Bits of the original stonework are visible in the reconstruction. Jonathan fingers them. From here the wall went south but the precise route is unclear. We track where it might have been, across Castle Street, between the cars and lunch-time shoppers, bending along Westgate Street. This was once the waterfront before the Taff was moved west. Jonathan has our walk down in his diary as a meeting. He takes business calls on his mobile as we go. Yes, black. Right. That was the builder working on the WMC glazing bars, he tells me. We stop at the blue plaque on the wall of the Westgate Street car park. This celebrates Blounts Gate, demolished 1785, named after its gatekeeper, access portal to the Town Quay. There's a note underneath which announces that the gate's foundations are marked somewhere inside the car park. The attendant is vague. Downstairs, mate. I've only seen them once in ten years and I work here. Maybe they're ghosts. Blount drifting in through them when the signs are right. Portal to the fog of the past. Step through it and you'll be there. But we find the foundations under a Nissan in the car park basement. A set of black bricks set at right angles to the course of the street. Blount's territory. I step across them. But time doesn't shift.

The wall moves on through invisible space, past the entrance to Glanmor's[28] Stadium, past the old Westgate Street Post Office, past the Queen's Vaults, to its next present day celebration – the blue plaque marking the Ship Gate or Gullygate, Porth y Longau, at the end of Frog Lane, the Golate today. Bugger all to do with sailors going late to their ships but rather the gate at the foot of the gully that once ran here. Water trickle, ash, town waste. And the last bit of quay before the mud and the sea. Not a dot on Speed's map to show that here a gate might have stood. No foundations found. All speculation. We walk on through the strong sunlight, past flower sellers and the marks on the rear wall of the Prince of Wales Wetherspoons showing where the end of St Mary's Church once was. Put there by a Victorian Architect at least a hundred years after the Church itself had fallen down. This is Great Western Lane. Beer being loaded into the back of Walkabout as we pass.

The site of the South Gate is simple to place. It was right there,

next to the traffic lights at the
end of St Mary Street, on
slightly raised ground where
the Great Western Hotel now
stands. North was the town,
south was mud, water meadow
and the sea. This was the Moor
Gate, the gate about which the
least is known. No discovered
foundations. A sketch on an old
map all that remains.

Following the wall north
from here is easy. As was the
way with mediaeval build the town fortifications were strengthened
by the addition of a "river", a moat of water running in the extended
trough from which the original vallum was dug. On the west it came
from the mill leat. On the east it was drained down from the Castle
moat. When the Glamorgan Canal was dug in 1796 its navigators
followed the line of this ditch almost exactly. You can see it on Wood's
1828 map. Jonathan waves his photocopy. We set off up the line along
The Hayes, through Cardiff's hopeful Café Quarter, past the
entrance to the Marriott. We reach the end of Bridge Street where the
map shows the wall turning slightly to the north and plunging
through reception at the slickly named Department of Work and
Pensions Inherited Serps. Progress barred. We pick up the line again
in Oxford Arcade and follow it north to where Frederick Street
emerges into Hills Street. Somewhere here once stood Cardiff's
eastern garret, Cock's Tower. Originally built to watch across the
moors "against the dangers of the sea"[29] but used in the fifteenth
century as a prison dungeon. Cardiff's Protestant martyr, Rawlins
White, was imprisoned here prior to his execution in 1555. It was the
tallest of the Town Wall's watchtowers and the longest lived. Parts still
stood in the nineteenth century. The Library has a photograph to
prove it. But like most things from ancient Cardiff there is now not a
trace. No plaque, no marks on the paving.

In an attempt to locate the tower precisely Jonathan has overlain on
computer an 1890s OS map with the present day equivalent. This
reveals that the tower did not stand on the flower bed outside
Waterstones as I had suspected but inside the rear of The Complete

Present. The owner, Paula Hutchinson, lets us take a look. We had the canal here, yes, but I don't know about any tower. Beyond the stacks of Cherished Teddies, Lilliput Lane Ceramic Cottages, Cascadia Art of Glass, engraved plates and slate carvings of King Arthur there it is. The staff toilets. Medieval prison, watchtower, martyr's death cell. unmarked, uncelebrated. The Cardiff tradition, it seems.

We've got Rawlins' ghost with us now as well as Blount's. Rawlins has God on his Walkman. Blount listens to mp3 sea shanties. We roll north up the St David's arcade. Are you sure the wall went here? asks Jonathan. That's the name of the Arcade, I tell him. Mur y Dref it says, helpfully, above the glass doors. From here it's simple. Jonathan talks of stepped walkways and return walls. Architectural pedimentia. We pass Clarks Shoes where the line of the wall is actually marked in the marble mall walkway. The route leads up Queen's Arcade to emerge on Queen Street itself opposite T.K. Maxx and Superdrug. The East Gate stood here. Under a JCB repairing Cardiff's services is a run of black paving which marks the site. This is where toy-mic Trevor usually stands to sing, in his fractured tenor, Only You into his battery-less plastic microphone. Not here today. Resting. We've seen nothing original yet, it's worth noting, only present day reminders. Even the Westgate was a Victorian replica. But using some original stone, says Jonathan. Maybe.

The line of the wall goes north up the Friary between JJB Sports and the Principality Building Society. It swings left where the north watch tower once stood outside present-day Bar Cuba. We head towards the Castle though the Queen's West get-in yard. Here, among the unloading lorries, wheelie dump bins and parked cars stands the only fragment of Cardiff's town wall still in place. It's a short section of around two meters high by four or five wide, heavily remortared, but distinctively old. There's evidence from a flat oval-shaped section of skim in the wall's centre that a plaque once hung here. Gone. We push through sprawled rubbish from Barfly for a closer view. Jonathan spots the new repairs – valley stones inserted within the past one hundred years. Above them more ancient material. River stone. Real Town Wall. This is now the rear of Bradford & Bingley. Round the front I ask Sian the receptionist if she knows that they've a slice of Cardiff history built into their premises. No. Didn't know Cardiff had a wall. Same story. Are you property developers? We are not. Jonathan asks who occupies the building's third floor. No one. Empty. Half of Cardiff's city centre must be like this. A dusty, echoing, empty slice of space laid over the bustle and commerce. Maybe we should make them an offer.

The wall returns to the Castle through the North gate which once straddled Kingsway. Sentry Gate. Senghenydd Gate. Pulled down in 1786. Nothing left. Some ancient masonry at the back of the raised flowerbed in the Castle moat. Evidence of efflorescence. Lime leach. Sign of age. It's taken around an hour and a half to walk the full circuit. No time. The past is so small. Jonathan heads off to meet a client. I browse the Castle bookshop where I find Steve Benbow's collection of City photographs[30]. Splendid technicolour. The present. The future. And of necessity. Cardiff's past has been stripped and washed so thoroughly clean that I begin to wonder if we might have invented it[31].

THE ROYAL

I'd loaned the book to George and he'd given it back to me with the corner of page twenty five turned down. Didn't get on with it, he said. It was my first inclination that there were people out there who never read. Good people. People whose lives would be enriched, if they did, who'd enjoy it. I knew. But when pressed they got as far as page twenty five and the threw the tiresome, mind-wrenching things down. The book in question was J.P. Donleavy's *The Ginger Man*, Corgi paper with the colophon of a dog with a book in its mouth, jacket worn, picked up from a stall in Bridge Street, second hand.

In his private life George was the mirror-image of *The Ginger Man*'s star, Sebastian Dangerfield. Loveable rogue. Drinker. Impoverished. Woman chaser, in luck, out of luck. Addled. Drunk. Why didn't he want to read about someone so like himself? But he didn't. Went instead in his Morris Marina rust bucket to liaisons with women in alleys down the docks. Pissed in the Dowlais. Falling down leaving the Casablanca. Reeling from the Philanderer. Scored every bloody time at the home of the brave, toughness personified, the sailor's best, the North Star.

J.P. Donleavy, the man himself, black overcoat, sucking a cigarette, tongues of shoes hanging out like hungry dogs, giving anything for a drink. Standing in the Dublin rain. Grey and wet and cold. Wearing

a rag of despair and sorrow. No money. Then a trickle from the book
sales. We'd have to get him over here. Cardiff like Dublin. Capitals.
Waterfronts. History of drunkenness and falling over. More Irish in
this town centre than Welsh in Liverpool. He'd come in a rush. New
books a-blazing. Joy up front at the prospect of meeting us local
scribblers. He would.

I wrote to the Arts Council and asked if they'd give me a grant and
they replied at length saying it was a classic idea and yes, I could have
half the costs so long as I raised the other half myself and then put on
a Welsh author the following week and, just to be a certain, another
Welsh writer the week before. I asked Glyn Jones if he'd do it, gentleman he always was, he said yes. Tom Earley, radical left, London
Welsh with a permanent desire to be asked back couldn't agree more
swiftly. It was a done deal. Glyn would speak to us rag bag poets at
No Walls upstairs at the Marchioness of Bute in Frederick Street. Tom
too. But for the creator of Sebastian Dangerfield we'd need something
better, bigger. The Royal Hotel, Captain Scott Room. Hallowed.
Large. Full of plush chairs and sofas.

The Royal Hotel, half way down St Mary Street, was enormous
when it was built in 1866. Five stories, stepped marble entrance,
columns, Victorian scale. The hotel was extended in 1890 to round
the corner into Wood Street. Stout columns of pink Aberdeen
granite. Horse carriages then later Bentleys would stop outside. For
decades a hotel in the grand manner. The great farewell dinner for
Captain Scott took place here in its lavish wood panelled first floor
ballroom in 1910. The following day, 15th June, Terra Nova sailed
from Cardiff for Antarctica, her crew never to return.

The Royal's Press Bar, letting onto Westgate Street through a
porch at the rear, was never much of a haunt for journalists from the
nearby *Echo* and *Mail* even if that's what it was intended for. Three
dinner ladies would sit on the bar stools each Friday pay day and get
pissed enough to fall off and apart from a smattering of lags and
dishevelled the rest of the bar was gay. In the hotel's cocktail lounge
beer came only in halves (to keep the riff-raff out) and men with
large signet rings and out of fashion blazers met divorcees in heels
and lace. The Captain Scott Room was above such ephemera. J.P.
agreed to come. He'd fly. Could he be met? I fixed it. Spent a slice of
the grant commissioning John Tripp, our own Sebastian Dangerfield
and the only literary man I could think of who'd be able to keep up

with the Ginger Man's drinking. I slipped him several fivers. Stay the course. Stand J.P. some drinks. Show him how good literary Wales is. You know where the dancing girls are? Tripp nodded. Go there.

In the event Donleavy turned out to be a tall, soft spoken gent in tweeds, brogues, waistcoat and walking stick. He insisted in being put up at The Park Hotel (it had a reputation). He drank whiskey (disliked beer). Singles. Refused our offers of hospitality (exhausted). Did his reading, took no questions and retired early. Polite applause. JT drank the pints he'd stacked himself. He kept what was left of the fivers for his trouble. I didn't get my copy of *The Ginger Man* signed, Donleavy disappeared too quickly. No coverage in the papers despite our location virtually overlooking the *Mail* newsroom. Writers in the seventies were not copy.

J.P. flew back to Dublin or caught the train to London the following day. I don't remember which. I'd asked George to come to the reading, offered him a free ticket, but he'd failed to show. Stuck in a bar somewhere else, couldn't get away. Just as well.

The ground floor of the Royal has now been gutted (apart from the glorious and listed single rise double return entrance staircase). One half is O'Neils the other Edwards. Bars. Full of light and lager. Welsh Sebastian Dangerfields. Ginger men and ginger girls.

Cardiff Arts (Old)

Wall hanging, dralon,
terylene, nylon,
lady with fish, fag-packet poodle,
Magistrates Court, cannons,
flowerbed feathers, rugs + carpets,
shipbits, dragons, daff on watertower,
St David's #2 man dancing,
embroidered rendition of miner's lamp,
print of elephant, glass fish, cart horse,
seascape sunset, Prince of Wales,
olde English script Roof Repairs,
Thatcher watercolour Con Club
City Road, Queen Street Xmas

illuminations (July), bus as loaf
of bread, haircut (Rhodri), all fountains,
Andrew Vicari public absence, metal bollocks
city hall, sloped brick main station,
flock wallpaper, rose beds, Attention This Vehicle
Is Reversing, rhif dau osgwelwch yn dda,
Oriel (closed), wall thing in the Castle Roman
Gallery, have you seen this, didn't think so.

ANGEL STREET

It's the eighteenth century. I'm in Angel Street. The paving is uneven,
houses back to back, mean and cottage like, clustering round into
tight Castle Street, more daub and wattle, wood and rough mortar
infill, bad brick stacked and stuck together with a limestone mix,
irregular angles, lollop and lean. I've come out of The Globe, beer
and warmth, into the Cardiff night. In 1877 these houses and the rest
of them, clustering for protection or warmth tight against the Castle
walls, were swept away in a fit of Bute-powered municipal town
planning. Cardiff was in a fit of change. Broad Street which wound
north between the Castle and the Taf was demolished. The Cardiff
Arms Hotel[32], straddling the street at right angles, was razed. A four
lane road way opened up, grass in front of the Castle, space and
breath. The Cardiff Arms licence went to the new Angel Hotel. The
land running to the back of it – the Little Park, the Drying Hayes –
became Cardiff Arms Park when Brunel shifted the course of the
river. The Globe, corner of Womanby Street, licensed 1731, rude and
rough, stayed on.

By the seventies, when Dave Reid was using it, that roughness had
been modified, but only a bit. Reid was a writer and bass guitarist,
blind from birth, family from Shrewsbury, working in Cardiff as a
piano tuner. He could tell light from dark and imagined that ringing
bells said *lawn dean* rather than *ding dong*. His mimicry was
legendary. Hear a voice once and next minute he could be that
person. On the phone to City Hall being George Thomas. Booking a
room at the Park as Richard Dimbleby. As Alistair Cook calling the
Chair of the Arts Council and demanding an interview "to discuss
the future", with special reference to poetry and those dams they'd

built drowning half of lovely
Wales. Reid, Kerouac's blind
Dean Moriarty, fuelling himself
ever further.

Reid's speciality was entering
a crowded pub in the company
of others and then blundering
blindly at the bar in a stumbling
rush. The usually recalcitrant
crowds would part for him like
the waters for Moses. He'd go
straight to the front and get
served immediately. Six pints
please. Certainly sir. A Jack Bruce disciple, he played electric bass for
the poetry and music band The Second Aeon Travelling Circus. This
position gave him a sort of Beat credibility, he imagined. Not that
he'd read much of the Beat Generation. He'd borrowed the red plastic
Fantasy album of Allen Ginsberg reading 'Howl', arranged for the
thirty-eight volume hard-bound Braille edition of *Ulysses* to be delivered to his flat in two full mail sacks[33] , and had various friends read
him extracts from *On The Road* and *The Naked Lunch*. So, you've got
to drink and take drugs to do it, he said to me. Visions. That's how it
happens. Ah yes.

As part of the Circus we travelled about a bit, usually in borrowed
vans, and mostly in a state of some intoxication. After one particularly
splendid performance at Merthyr and the party which followed[34], Reid
became difficult. The Beats, he'd decided, were charlatans. Their
visions were fantasy. Wales didn't need them. He'd wasted his time. It
was my fault. I'd told him that they were essential and clearly they
weren't. He took a blind swing at me, missed, and fell down the stairs.
We took him to the van where the fisticuffs continued. Bloody
Kerouac. Scuffle. Sod Burroughs. Thump. Roger, the driver, thought
the whole thing totally unfair. A sighted man and a blind one bashing
each other. The odds had to be evened. He drove us to the nearby
Beacons and pushed us out into the gorse. We stumbled and thrashed
about. There was no moon and no street light. Just stars. The fight was
equal at last. No one won, of course. I think Reid got stuck in a gully
and had to be pulled out while I got lost in the bushes. This is what
you did when you were a writer. Got lost, fought. It was there, in the

books. The future from then on turned to Thomas. The three of them: Dylan, Edward and R.S. Different sort of vision, less fighting but often still lost. Reid took a particular interest in Dylan.

Outside The Globe Reid is lying on the floor thrashing his white stick about and shouting. He's had eight pints, maybe, and feels he should be home but is unsure in which direction that is. It's two am and, in seventies Cardiff, most of the centre premises are shut down and dark. His stick connects with a window and a building alarm starts to clang satisfactorily. Within a short space of time the police have arrived, picked Reid up off the floor, and discovered that he's blind. They don't take him to cells with the other drunks but, instead, run him home to his flat at the top end of Cathedral Road. A special service for those who can't see. Reid stops shouting. Mission accomplished[35]. Calm returns to Angel Street. For a while.

In the eighties The Globe changed its name to The Four Bars and tried its luck as a jazz and poetry venue, with mixed results. Pubs in city centres constantly re-invent themselves. The problem was that, as a pub, the Four Bars was a haven for the lumpen ugly, the doped, the broken and the catastrophically drunk. Events were regularly interrupted by tattooed no-hopers shouting from doorways or falling off chairs. The poetry or jazz that got performed did so in an environment of risk. Creativity came face to face with gritty irrelevance. This was how cities were. Things flourished. Until the world moved on, that is, and creativity lost its avant garde front to become an expected norm. The room got double booked. The number of drunks increased. Jazzers gave up. Lost interest. Poetry moved to the Great Western at the bottom of St Mary Street. Jazz went to the Sandringham. The Four Bars rebranded itself as Dempseys. Irish was in. For a time.

Dave Reid[36] eventually succeeded as a musician. Made some records as bass player for the Welsh singer Meic Stevens. Abandoned the Four Bars, made a little cash.

Outside there's no sign left of Angel Street. This front of Castle roadway is now known as Castle Street. The section to the right of High Street is called Duke Street. No residences, all shops, banks, offices. At two am the place is still jumping. Lie on the floor and flail a stick about and people will just step over you. The alarms won't go off, they are too sophisticated. But are the passers-by intoxicated? You bet they are.

SORTING WORKING STREET

It's a Saturday in 1970 and I'm heading north from Spillers on the
Hayes. Spillers, home of the hits for decades and still there, is
Cardiff's pre-eminent independent record trader. It was founded by
Henry Spiller in 1894 selling musical instruments and sheet Music
and was one of the first places anywhere to retail the new recorded
music – wax cylinders, shellac 78s – and the machines that went with
them. Today it concentrates on the music – CDs for less than a tenner
– acid-house, alt. country, rock and techno. In the 70s you went there
for psychedelia, folk rock, and for r&b – the real stuff: Jimmy Reed,
Sonny, Muddy, John Lee Hooker, harmonicas, twelve-bar.

I've passed Hills Street with warm, welcoming City Radio.
Checked there earlier, couldn't find the Airplane. Stood racking
through the vinyl, smoking. Maurice, the owner, put an ash tray
disapprovingly on the bin next to me. Said nothing. Next Woolworths
and a slip through their own-label Embassy hit replicas. Half the
price of the authentic but recorded by imitators. I spend the whole
afternoon like this. Record shop to record shop. Sitting in the glass
booth listening to Moby Grape, The Dead, The Doors, Quicksilver
Messenger Service, Neil Young, Buffalo Springfield. I caught Victor
Freed when they closed their shop at No 6 Duke Street and bought
up a great stack of CBS singles for a shilling each. Dylan, Spirit,
Byrds. Filled the gaps. 'Can You Please Crawl Out Your Window'[37].
Who'd heard of that?

Along Working Street are the guys in loon pants. Flapping cheese-
cloth shirts. Beads and love outside St John's. The graveyard not
cleared and turned to park yet. Still full of winos drinking, winos
shouting, winos reclining. The church with its Norman tower, seeped
with age, stripped inside. But still a church with a congregation and
still active. Inner city parish. Climb the tower. Proceeds to the roof
fund. Did it then, 1970. Did it again 2004.

Peace and love and the whole psychedelic generation impinged less
on Cardiff than it could have. Despite enlightenment in the arts –
sculpture shows in the grounds of the Castle and new-gen poster art
– Allen Jones, Jeffrey Steele and Terry Setch – put up on giant bill
boards around the city – the Mark Boyle light shows and streets full
of incense and bubbles failed to completely materialise. Saturday,
1970. A year after Woodstock. A year after the Rolling Stones debacle

at Altamont[38] when peace and love finally beached itself. But in Cardiff it still felt like a suburban 1967. Time stilled. Beads on the streets. Someone coming out of C&A wearing a kaftan made from his mother's braided curtains. Two greasers in ice-blues walking down from Queen Street Station. A bunch of parka-wearing *Sanity* sellers outside the Library. No one with a tattoo apart from the street-stall veg sellers. We are the people our parents warned us against. Sure.

I've got the Airplane's *Volunteers* under my arm. Recorded at the tired end of 1969 and released here in 1970. Great gate-fold sleeve with the band as a mask-wearing anarchist army on the front; a giant peanut butter sandwich inside. The Jefferson Airplane (note Airplane not Aeroplane, which is how most of us pronounced it) were the hottest point to the San Francisco Haight Ashbury renaissance. They were the band that made the glory I held in my hand. *Volunteers* – did anyone else in Cardiff own a copy? My Guess was no. The Airplane had been on everyone's players in '67 with White Rabbit and Somebody to Love. In the dives where blue fluorescent shone your teeth and picked out the dandruff on your shoulders they played constantly. But British Maharishi consciousness, beads and flowers, had somehow looped around them. Volunteers, the greatest rock album of the period, had gone unremarked. Who is the best guitarist? Clearly the Airplane's Jorma Kaukonen (just listen to him on 'Good Shepherd', soaring from speaker to speaker). In Cardiff, however, the fans preferred the Shadows' Hank Marvin.

Volunteers was a rallying call come too late. Look what's happening on the streets. Got a revolution. On 'Wooden Ships', the Airplane outdid Crosby, Stills and Nash. On 'Hey Fredrick' Kaukonen's guitar rampage showed Clapton how it should be done. Holding the album I imagined myself part of something that could actually change things. We'd be there, in the positions of power, by the end of the decade. The dead hand of unenlightened authority would wither. The world would be different, our world, as we wanted it. But it wouldn't be, of course. It would end up the same, or worse, still full of greed, death and corruption.

'Eskimo Blue Day' did not get radio airtime. 'We Can Be Together' was not played in the discos. No pub rock band felt concerned to try 'Good Shepherd'. Not that there were many such bands. This was south Wales, 1970. Nothing had happened yet. Although I didn't realise it then this was the Airplane's highspot. For the rest of the '70s they'd be wrecked by heroin, rolled by speed. Wracked by boundless egos. Fooled by madness. Believing Kantner's insistence that they would somehow fly to the moon, the band slowly declined. There were great projects and wonderful moments en-route. 'Sunfighter', the Slick-Kantner SF extravaganza. *Blows Against The Empire*, where the band had renamed itself the Jefferson Starship. Bark. Barron Von Tollbooth and the Chrome Nun. But their flight was still down.

At the top of Working Street the road opens out into St John's Square. Full of traffic. A Wimpy Bar where you get waitress service. Slow burgers. From then until now everything gets progressively faster. The tag Jefferson got dropped. The Starship flew then blew up in a ball of unnoticed fire. They've got stacks of their records in the racks of Kelly's Second Hand, upstairs in the indoor market. But they aren't worth listening too. Grace Slick has retired. Nothing more unpalatable than a woman in her 60s dancing round the stage like a teenager, she's reported as saying. Had a revolution. Now it's gone.

Cardiff Haiku

half a bike
in the East Dock
It was there last year

Chrysanthemums in the
Mansion House window
Cleaner has been

On the roaring drinkers
In the lower city
Night rain

Moon fleeting fast
Dragon flags on the castle
no fire in sight

Sound of clock chime
Fills his sandwiches
In the lunchtime park

Ah, plum blossom
City hall ringed daily
By abandoned cars

We vote silently
While the councillor singing
Shows us his arse

notes

1. Howells – James Howells' great department store – first established under Stuart Hall in the Hayes in 1865. The company was taken over and re-badged by House of Fraser in the latter part of the twentieth century.
2. Rice Merrick, in 1578, calls the Gild Hall the 'Bothall'. This was the town's civic centre with court-room, town bell, town clock and a town shambles (meat market), and Cockmoil below. The Cockmoil (in Welsh Cwchmoel) was the town prison. At its lower end stood the town stocks, the town pump, the town cross and the town great stone. There were places to leave your horse and a Wednesday and Saturday market. Medieval Cardiff had everything to hand, all at its centre.
3. Wetherspoons' Prince of Wales was first the Theatre Royal (1878), renamed the Prince of Wales Theatre later to become a cinema (with a penchant for the sub-titled, 50s horror and b&w nudist extravaganzas), then a casino and finally a loosely regulated night club. It was redeveloped as Wales' largest pub in the 1990s. The building occupies a site that was formerly part of St Mary's Churchyard.
4. The town in the late eighteenth century had a population of less than 2000 who were serviced by 27 public houses. Enough is enough, said the Licensing Justices. Things have since changed.
5. Now the Taurus Steak House
6. Valley Lines Poetry – a series of six poems made as posters and mounted in the style of Poems on the Underground on Valley Line Trains (now run by Arriva) to mark the tenth anniversary of the University of Glamorgan. The poets, intellectual heavyweights and versifiers of some reputation, include Matthew Francis, Tony Curtis, Sheenagh Pugh, Meic Stephens, Jeremy Hooker and Chris Meredith. They are all members of the University's English Department. The scheme was launched to great acclaim with blanket south Wales media coverage and the suggestion that these poets would now be travelling on early morning trains in and out of Treforest declaiming their verses to half-asleep commuters. An Anglo-Welsh breakthrough. But in reality the launch took place in a siding and after the flashguns had finished the participants returned to their classes. Matthew Francis' poem 'Invocation' quoted above comes from his Faber collection *Dragons* (2001)
7. The Spital was the town's medieval leper hospital and is shown on Speeds map of Cardiff (1610) outside the walls at the eastern end of what he calls Cokkerton Street (now Queen Street). The hospital with its 24 beds was founded early in the thirteenth century when leprosy was the Aids of the age. It was succeeded by an early version of Cardiff's Royal Infirmary and later by Spital Buildings. The site is now occupied by Sainsbury's Metro. The Rhymney Railway's station at the end of The Parade was built on the site of the Spittal's barn.
8. From 'Daearyddiaeth', Oliver Reynolds (originally published in his *Skevington's Daughter*, Faber & Faber, 1985)

9. Described in depth in his *Welsh Fever – Welsh Activities in the United States and Canada Today*, D Brown & Sons Ltd., 1986.

10. *Undeb* is the Welsh for Union. A word that gets us together. For years another Undeb was an amateur football team from Cardiff with not one Welsh speaker among its players. The boys universally mispronounced their name as un deb. In late 2003, unable to balance the books, the Womanby Street enterprise went into free fall and has now re-opened as *Sugar*, a non-membership restaurant and bar.

11. Grahame's poems which brilliantly describe Welsh life in the Capital can be found in *Cadwyni Rhyddid*, Cyhoeddiadau Barddas, 2001. The volume won the prestigious Arts Council Book of the Year Award.

12. Y Rhath (Roath), Llys-faen (Lisvane), Rhymni (Rumney), Treganna (Canton) and Yr Eglwys Newydd (Whitchurch).

13. Abse, Dannie, *Ash On A Young Man's Sleeve*, Hutchinson, 1954.

14. Picton, Bernard (Bernard Knight), *Tiger At Bay*, Robert Hale, 1970.

15. John Williams, 'Cardiff Bred', article for the *Western Mail* (unpublished).

16. Hawes, James, *White Powder, Green Light*, Cape 2002.

17. Williams, John, *Five Pubs, Two Bars and a Nightclub*, Bloomsbury, 1999; *Cardiff Dead*, Bloomsbury, 2000; *The Prince of Wales*, Bloomsbury, 2003.

18. Burke, Sean, *Deadwater*, Serpent's Tail, 2002.

19. Davis, Anna, *Melting*, Hodder & Stoughton, 2000.

20. James, Bill, *Middleman*, *The Do Not Press*, 2002.

21. Robson, Lloyd, *Cardiff Cut*, Parthian Books, 2001.

22. Brito, Leonora, *Dat's Love*, Seren, 1995.

23. Williams, Herbert, *Punters*, Gomer, 2002.

24. Azzopardi, Trezza, *The Hiding Place*, Picador, 2000.

25. John Speed (1552-1629) published the first ever cartographic record for the whole of the British Isles. His *Theatre of the Empire of Great Britain* contained 67 maps covering the counties of England, Wales and Ireland. His maps were based on surveys carried out by Christopher Saxton, John Norden and William Smith. In Wales his surveys were made by Gerard Mercator. In the corners of each county map Speed included a detail of a principle town. His map for Glamorgan shows Cardiff and Llandaff. GLAMORGANSHYRE WITH THE SITUATIONS OF THE CHIEFE TOWNE CARDYFF AND ANCIENT LLANDAFF DESCRIBED. His drawings show in relief houses, gardens, trees. You can still buy Speed's maps. Reproductions will cost a few pounds. A original will set you back £600.

26. So called because of its proximity to the town mills which stood nearby.

27. Rice Merrick refers to the West Gate as the Miskin Gate, the road through it leading to Miscin, Llantrisant.

28. Glanmor Griffiths, Chief Executive of the WRU (rtd.)

29. William Jenkins, *History of the Town and Castle of Cardiff*, 1854.

30. *Cardiff / Caerdydd*, Graffeg, 2003.

31. Visit web.onetel.net.uk/~herbertroese/med.htm to read Historian Herbert Roese's excellent website devoted to the wall. Jonathan and I are not the only fanatics.

32. The Cardiff Arms Hotel stood on the site of an earlier inn – Ty Coch – which first got its licence in 1710. Knock down Cardiff drinkers and they'll bounce right back.

33. It's Beat isn't it? No, not really. Well, it'll do.

34. Hosted by Harri Webb at the legendary Garth Newydd.

35. It didn't always work out like this. On one occasion Reid, enormously the wrong side of eight pints and with other substances co-mingling in his system, exited again from his Cathedral Road flat after having been returned there, to continue shouting and thrashing about in the road. When the police returned they took him in. Drunk and disorderly. £20 fine. Don't do it again. No sir.

36. Dave Reid died of heart failure while playing in America in 2002.
37. 'Can You Please Crawl Out Your Window' – Bob Dylan. Single released 1965, sank without a trace – never included on a contemporary album. Collected on *Biograph* in 1985
38. Altamont, outside San Francisco, California was the venue for the great Rolling Stones Gimme Shelter tour. A free concert at a speedway stadium featuring Santana, the Grateful Dead, Jefferson Airplane, Crosby Stills Nash and Young, the Flying Burrito Brothers, and Mick Jagger's arrogant, biker-championing Stones. The Stones took it upon themselves to hire local Hell's Angels as security and instead of love, dope and understanding got drink, acid and violence. The Angels beat their way forward using beer cans and pool cues. There were four deaths and a great raft of diabolical egoism. The age of freedom and under-standing had come to an end. Check *Minnesota Echoes*, Adam Stanley's analysis of over twenty years of American music festivals at www.echoes.com/rememberaday/index.html for much more detail.

WEST

THE BRIDGE OVER THE CANNA

We're making our way through the beech and ash thicket looking for a watercourse. Among the fallen branches and undergrowth of ivy and ground elder Grahame Davies has found the remains of a medieval bridge. It's half submerged in the undergrowth and massive. Conclusive proof if ever we needed it. But on investigation it turns out to be a tumbled remnant of the boundary wall from a property on the Penhill ridge above. The breeze blocks give it away. Discovery defeated.

We're in Llandaf Fields looking for the Canna. The white brook that gave its name to a large part of upwardly mobile north Canton. Despite a whole load of smoke about it being a saint's name, holy relics at St Tudor's Mynyddislwyn, and ley lines jetting through Canton Cross on their way to Mars, *Canna* is far more likely to be simply the Welsh for *to whiten*. As usual I've got a bag of photocopies of old maps with me. The 1840[1] shows Nant-y-Ty-Gwyn (The White House Brook) rising somewhere below the Penhill ridge and then snaking south to join the Taff opposite what's now the Millennium Stadium. There's an overgrown ditch at this spot but it's dry. We follow it north. Grahame is talking about his novel. Inspiration is arriving at the most inconvenient of moments but the thing is demanding to be written. He's already done 25,000 words, most of them after midnight. The best work always gets done under pressure. Books jamming themselves into the corners of their author's lives. Plots hammering around the table at breakfast. William Golding completed *Lord of the Flies* in a flat above a chip shop. He had a young

family squalling around him and wrote after teaching all day to pay the rent. There's a message here. Grahame's book is bubbling out of him rather like the Canna ought to be from the ground we're surveying. It's about a young Welsh nationalist who keeps the faith while the world around her slides into post-devolutionary torpor. She's naïve, unworldly, guileless and outmanoeuvred by her Labour

PROBABLE ROUTE OF THE CANNA

opponents. She's a metaphor for the nationalist movement as a whole. What happens to her? Grahame is not telling.

Eventually we discover a fenced-in spread of marsh just below Penhill's Pontcanna Court. There's an obligatory milk crate sinking into its wet centre. The Canna's ancient source? Could be. Pont Canna[2] derives its name from the bridge that reputedly once crossed the whitening stream. Historical sources[3] claim this to have been situated near Pontcanna Cottages. These were a short thatched row that stood, until 1896, between the former Presbyterian Church on Cathedral Road and Teilo Street. Photographs exist and the dwellings are there on all the maps[4]. But of the Canna at that point and its mythical bridge? Not a sign.

If the Whitehouse Brook and the Canna were the same thing, and that seems likely, then the watercourse would have crossed Pen-Hill Road and headed south in the direction of the Conway public house. Grahame spots a green lane to the back of Llanfair Road with an obvious water relic along its route – an ancient mill. But it's not. It's a garage. Foiled again. Maybe we should come down here with a hazel twig and try water divining.

This whole area of upper Canton has been progressively gentrified. Victorian mansions have had their fifties modernisations ripped out and original clawfoot baths, dressers, newel posts, and pewter door knobs reinstalled. Gardens have been tended, roofs fixed, doors re-knockered and re-painted. Prices have risen like apricot sponge.

We pass the late John Ormond's house along Conway Road and go round the corner into Romilly Crescent. The district has immaculate credentials. Behind the Urdd is St Winifreds Nursing Home. Both Saunders Lewis and George Thomas died there. Sun leaks through the plane trees. Is the Canna still here, deep below us in the City drains? Does it rise when the rain comes to return as street flood, dampening people's cellars, swarming up their brick-work and drawing maps on their wallpaper? Can you hear it, in the sewers, heading towards the sea? Wyndham Crescent is dust dry. Dead leaves. Dying grass. Water a memory.

Some records talk of the streams that were once here being the Turton and the Glas, minor tributaries of the Canna, trickling in from Canton Pool and Plas Turton, the great house that preceded Plasturton Gardens. Maybe the area was once a flood plain criss-

crossed by damp ditches and alluvial sludge. As we walk south the nature of the district begins to change. Houses are closer together, smaller yards, flaky paintwork, less refurbishment. Locals I've spoken to know nothing of the river that once flowed beneath them. But dampness, yes, that they do recognise. Wallpaper comes off. Skirtings need replacing. There's salt in the mortar.

At the border, Canton Bingo on Cowbridge Road, the unofficial district of Pontcanna officially ends. CV'S & TYPING – Premier Business Services – Gardian Property Management – Secura Windows. The Balti Wallah Punjabi Tandoori. The historian William Rees talks of a bridge here which once crossed the Canna at the King's Castle[5]. Long gone.

Grahame is explaining to me how a single shrieker is all you need among a poetry reading audience in order to get the whole crowd going. If they enjoy themselves then they'll buy the book. Smile and the world smiles with you. Rocet Jones did this at the Coopers' Arms on Grahame and Lloyd Robson's Cymru Cut tour of 2002. Grahame shifted a shed of his *Cadwyni Rhyddid* and Lloyd sold dozens of *Cardiff Cut* as a result. We cross the road. Make them laugh. Obvious really. We pass the back of Mandeville House and turn into Brook Street, on its corner The Miller's Arms, beer, breakfast, b&b. Here were actual mills, once, just south west of the castle. A town enterprise, reputed to charge more to grind your corn than anyone further out. You want to lug your grain to Llandaf where it's a penny a sack cheaper, you do it squire. Nothing changes. I ask someone unloading their Escort if there's a brook still here. No idea, sorry.

Before it degraded into a damp ditch[6] with its power gone and its waters dispersed though a hundred new Canton drains the Canna went along here. It rushed into the Taff in foaming leap. Doesn't now. Although there is a pipe half way down the stone reinforced river embankment. Under its corroded lid we find damp street detritus, crisp packets, mud and debris. The Canna, what's left, a memory of a trickle.

NORTH RIVERSIDE

I met Fifi in an internet chatroom. Friendly, open to suggestion, keen. She thought that I'd spent too much of my life in Roath and that I

should get out more. Whatever you think of Pontcanna and its
denizens, she wrote, its dramatic conversion into media land deserves
at least a mention. She'd read *Real Cardiff*, clearly. In that book
Pontcanna got scant coverage. A bit about Chapter, a cameo on the
King's castle. Reviewing it James Hawes said this wasn't enough. He
should know. The vehicle Fifi and I were using for our exchange was
the weblog of Badly Dubbed Boy (BDB), a Cardiff-based internet
geek who is systematically engaged in putting his entire life on-line.
He'd been complaining that multi-racial Cardiff was, in fact, a bit of
a myth. "Everyone's just slapping themselves on the back about how
multi-cultural they are, on the basis they know bhangra is not a
boxing event" ran one weblog entry. Fifi's response was to say that,
as a Jewish Yorkshirewoman, she felt very multi-cultural in Cardiff.
Just the guide I needed. Walk me round the district? Why not.

Fifi turns out to be Viv Goldberg, a content producer for BBC new
media. We meet at Pontcanna's southern extremity, outside St Mary of
the Angels on the corner of Talbot Street and King's Road, a Catholic
testament to the district's Irish origins. Vincent Kane once lived near
here and still attends. According to the Council, Viv tells me,
Pontcanna does not exist. This is North Riverside. West Cardiff. Fields
until the eighteen-sixties. Now solid housing with hardly a chink of
green. The main artery, Cathedral Road, running from Plasturton
farm at the bottom to Pontcanna Farm at the top, was originally
known as Pontcanna Lane. It was developed at the high Victorian end
of the nineteenth century and was the home of well-to-do merchants,
ship owners, and the wealthiest of Cardiff business families. The
houses, some lost to redevelopment at the city end, are architectural
classics. Their grandeur, if slightly faded, is palpable. At the bottom are
the three domes of the United Synagogue, the inspiration of Colonel
Albert Goldsmid, and centre for Cardiff Jews until faith transferred to
Cyncoed in 1989. It's now a business centre, but the conversion has
left the original architecture by Delissa Joseph largely intact.

Fifi tells me that her straw-poll research among local luvvies has
come up with a Pontcanna boundary line that runs from Pen-Hill via
Llandaf Fields and Cathedral Road to Hamilton Street and then up
King's Road, Romilly Crescent and Conway Road back to Pen-Hill.
You can tell when you've crossed it from that new indicator of class,
an increase in the density of on-street litter coupled with a dramatic
fall in the use of green bags. Media-types started to move in when by

nice co-incidence in the sixties the BBC transferred from Stacey Road in Roath to new studios in Llandaf, and TWW (later HTV) built theirs on ground at the edge of Pontcanna Fields. Cardiff was suddenly a media capital. TV acquired 625 lines and colour. Every home had to have one. Producers, writers, directors, stars and catering staff arrived in droves. When S4C was established in the eighties its first base was on the edge of Sophia Gardens. Small media companies clustered around it. Pontcanna painted its windows, stripped its pine doors, sand-blasted its stonework and shot up in price.

One of the great joys of the area is the lack of uniformity among its houses. The leasehold system, on which most of Cardiff was originally built, encouraged bulk build and a housing stock of uniform size and appearance. But in the one significant freehold development, centred according to the historian John Davies around Severn Grove, builders did what they wanted. Plots were of differing sizes, structures were singular, and the resultant Edwardian melee was a complete pleasure. Fifi points out what she calls the Karl Marx houses in Kings Road – a string of three terraces encrusted with an overkill of brightly painted decorative stucco and topped over each doorway with a bearded, long moustachioed and significantly eye-browed staring face reminiscent of the great thinker. Ed Thomas territory. Further up towards Pontcanna's hub, at the junction of King's Road and Pontcanna Street, the incidence of Welsh sign-boarding increases. High density cymraeg is a feature of the media industry. Comes with the territory. Jon Gower, Grahame Davies, Nia Ceidiog, John Pierce Jones, Jim Jones, Manon Rhys, Wiliam Owen Roberts, Elinor Wyn Reynolds live here. The Mochyn Du offers bi-lingual beer. Even the launderette on Pontcanna Street advertises its services in Welsh.

So who else is famous around here, Fifi? Dennis O'Neill's brother. Come to that Dennis O'Neill himself still has a house. Cerys Matthews once. And Van Morrison. But discount that rumour, it's an urban myth.

At the heart of Pontcanna sits the Cameo Club (members only, improved enormously in recent years), Café Brava and Cibo where locals do brunch on Sunday and discuss scripts and other media projects for most of the rest of the week. There are two barbers, Shelley's famous deli, frame shops, high-class children's toys, Caban Siop Llyfrau Cymraeg. South used to lie Pontcanna Old Books, the most exciting antiquarian shambles in Wales, maps, gems, aged bargains. Gone. Replaced with, One Pontcanna Street, a Bauhaus coffee shop that is rumoured to also be an architectural practice. The best restaurant in Cardiff, Le Gallois – Y Cymro, is in Romilly Crescent. This is the media-types' eatery of choice and is lampooned for being so in *White Powder, Green Light*[7]. But who cares, the food is brilliant.

We walk past heading for the old HTV studios at Fields Park Road, now red-brick housing. The Electricity Club, still rocking (PLEASE LEAVE QUIETLY THROUGH THE RESIDENTIAL AREA). Pontcanna Fields, vast and green. Lone golfers, riding school, caravan club. The old mill leat from Llandaf once crossed here to empty in the Taf. A bridge ran over it, another pont in Pontcanna. The long filled-in open-air swimming baths, much frequented by paralytic Conway drinkers, were here. And there's the Ride, Lon Lâs Cymru, the slightly raised, densely-avenued path which runs straight and very long from the Glamorgan County Cricket ground at the top of Sophia Gardens to Western Avenue. Estate agents celebrate this space when they sell their properties. "Near wonderful Pontcanna Fields. Cardiff's green lung. Walk to the city centre without once using a road. In autumn the sight is unrivalled. Welsh New England." All true, these remarks. And to the price they add several thousand. Peace. Space.

On the return walk we pass a sign advertising African Hand Drumming classes in King's Road, a diversion for the middle classes. Plasturton Gardens, a small iron fenced spread of lime and birch leaf, mahonia and cotoneaster scrub, bench and planting reminds me of an inner-city London park. Space for boules. There ought to be a basket-ball net, rash of cans and plastic waste, bust seating. But there isn't.

High on a house wall at the south end of King's Road is a painted sign – Est 1898 C.E.WATTS Boot Repairing DEPOT. This is one of Pontcanna's southern boundaries. Cardboard boxes and tumbling trash on the pavement outside. What else.

SIX PUBS AND A CHIP SHOP

There's a whole marketing industry working hard to push us in drink's direction. Kingsley Amis reckoned that most of it was twaddle. The only promotion that alcohol ever needed was a large sign saying BEER MAKES YOU DRUNK. There wasn't one outside the Half Way. But it did say BRAINS and that was enough. The Half Way, corner of William Street and Cathedral Road, is half-way into the city or half-way out of it, I'm not sure which. An apparently unreconstructed working-class pub that's served its time as a resting place for HTV liggers when the studios used to be round the corner and for sweating rugby players fresh from running on Llandaf Fields. From a distance it looks the same as it always did. Inside, however, it's clear that reconstruction has occurred. A Brains version of ash, chrome and aluminium contemporaneity without actually using any of those materials. Welsh drinkers noir. Perfect. The bar, snug, smoke room and lounge have been opened into one flowing heave of drinking: new dark wood, big clear glass windows, no signs saying PORT AND FINE ALES anywhere. I order a half of dark, just to keep in touch, and watch the Saturday night melée build up steam. Troops of women with bare midriffs, tattoos of leprechauns and other celtic nonsense sneaking up into view above the tops of their knickers. A rush of blokes wearing knee socks, caps and coloured sweaters fills the lower section. New age morris dancers or collectors for an obscure charity? Everyone is under thirty. You start at the Half Way and continue elsewhere. Us too.

The idea behind the escapade is to round out the polished chrome and sand-blasted Victoriana view I have of Pontcanna by trekking through some of its pubs at a time when they are likely to be full. The Conway Hotel, staggering distance round the corner, was once the Welsh centre of the western Cardiff universe. In the seventies when cymraeg was regarded by most Cardiffians as the territory of phoneys, farmers, and fanatics the Conway was a safe haven. *Un peint, dau beint, tri pheint* you could slur at the bar staff, mutating perfectly, and be understood. In fact Welsh learners from the nearby Aelwyd yr Urdd could only get served if they did mutate correctly. Ask for *dau peint* and the bar staff would move on to serve someone else. The locals held court in the front bar, the learners in the back. The lounge, in a sort of outbuilding on Mortimer Road, was only ever opened on special occasions. All changed now.

Like the Half Way the Conway has opened itself up into a long single drinking area that rolls in a loping right-handed bend around the central bars. Drinking is like agriculture. Economic return is greater in larger spaces. The Conway has gone in for middle-class home comfort. Open fires, stuffed sofas, discrete lighting, newspapers, shelves of books and toys and games. And real beer too. I have Brains Dark Red which is a new one on me but turns out to be indistinguishable other than by enhancement of its name from regular Dark. There is a rumour about, these days, that you can actually stay at the Conway too. Outside is a chalk board bearing the words RUGBY SPECIAL – CONTINENTAL BREAKFAST – Tea & Coffee, 3 Pints of Draught – £10. But we have a plan and a route and through the firework darkness (it's November, month of spark and rocket and endless bangs) we move on.

A swift slide through falling leaves along the very mixed residential architecture of Conway Road itself takes us to Romilly Crescent, land of great restaurants, car radio repair and the Romilly Hotel. Repainted outside, bashed about in, it's full of smoke and old soul music. Enough space, easy to sit and drink. The Board behind the counter announces Hot Pot, Pie, Peas and Gravy served until 9.00. But this is Saturday so it's off. The floor is carpeted, ceiling low, and there are thick curtains. All of this serves to deaden the echo and shout which fills most of Brains' pubs. The big difference between Brains and the enterprises of other breweries, of course, is in the speed of service. At a Brains enterprise it's inevitably white hot. My companion asks what real ale they have. Carlsberg. No, real ale. Well there's Carling, and Smoothflow and Guinness. The barman points at the pumps. CAMRA have not done their work here yet. Behind him four cheese and ham baps sit wrapped in tight clingfilm as if they were slimming. We have half of bitter and crisps and sit at a huge brown wooden table, large enough for a meeting of United Nations.

Quiz night was in the week. Karaoke? Not really. Someone with a hippie pony tail sings along to a version of Scott McKenzie's 'San Francisco' ("Wear Some Flowers In Your Hair") performed by the Big Ben's Banjo Band. Just one of six million tracks available on the enormous jukebox. Reality is on hold here – the present vague. The past somehow neutered. The Wilton dragging on your shoes.

At the Robin Hood in Severn Grove it's a completely different story. Here, in this magnificent double entranced, pillar and finial fronted and utterly unrebuilt slice of the sixties past, reality is running strong. We arrive just as the advertised Saturday night music bangs into the smoke-filled air. Black-clad George Jones, his lead guitarist, drum machine, microphones and amplifiers occupy almost a quarter of the bar. George is dressed in black. The lead guitarist wears a grey wig. The music is perfect for the place. Chuck Berry with the edges knocked off, filtered through Dire Straits. The irregular-looking regulars could be extras in a Tyneside television drama. But this is south Wales. An overweight woman of indeterminate age sways back from the security of the bar to boogie between the tables. A completely plastered fifty-year old, still in his dust covered working clothes, sings along, wrong words, big arm stretches like he was on stage. In one hand a fag, in the other a pint. Behind me someone wearing an ancient waistcoat, tight striped shirt, rounded collar, tie and home-barbered salt and pepper hair downs a bottle of Newcastle Brown. Hardly anyone seems to have bothered to shave. Is it like this every night? I ask an ancient in a creased bomber jacket and Oxfam trousers. Mnnnghgh ghh, he replies. Would buying him a drink elicit more information? Probably not.

The route down Cathedral Road to the Cayo Arms is made to deviate via Pete's Plaice for chips and gravy. The Clarks Pies sell out by seven. It's now nine-thirty. What did I expect? On the wall are notices reminding us not to bring our bikes in or to sit on the shelf, it might collapse. Behind the counter is a tea towel with the words of the All Black's Haka in English. "One upwards step! Another upwards step! The sun shines!". Outside it certainly does not.

The Cayo Arms is a new venture built into a converted Cathedral Road Victorian residence. No history other than that which it has appropriated by calling itself after the late William Edward Julian Cayo-Evans, Commandant of the Free Wales Army. The Bomber's Arms. Are there flags, republican slogans and explosives equipment decorating the place? No. But his face is there, moustachioed and smiling, on the new pub sign. Inside it's wide tabled contemporary with a huge pre-painted menu chalk board dominating one wall. There are loads of decent beers (including Tomos Watkin's famous OSB) and a brisk trade in Saturday night tipsiness that gets no where near that experienced earlier at the Robin Hood. We sit at the back amid a slurry of fag ash, uneaten peanuts, crisp fragments and beer mat pulp. The Cayo is, like The Halfway, not somewhere you go but somewhere you pass through. We've arrived after everyone else has left. The piped music is disco something lost in the wash of pub talk, all of which seems to be in English. I hunt around for characters, deviants, eccentrics, the famous, the smashed. But there are none.

Y Mochyn Du (The Black Pig), round the corner in Sophia Close on the way to the National Sports Centre, was formerly called The Lodge and before that actually was a lodge at the gateway to the wife of Lord Bute's eponymous gardens. Today it's a pub with superior bar meals, a large beer garden, some excellent ale and is probably the Welshest boozer in Caerdydd. As we stumble through the door I bump into Jim Jones, crowned bard, and almost as plastered as I am, although much better at standing up. I need to sit. We manage to squeeze in at the back of a gaggle of cuddly women in halter tops, bloopy bejewelled midriffs and wearing battery-illuminated plastic fobs round their necks. They are talking about the bar they intend to roll on to next (we're now a mere ten minutes from the city centre) but show no sign of moving yet. The décor is round tables, loads of ceiling height, ash floor. Clwb Werin Sesiwn Fach in the week. Welsh learners suppers on Mondays. West Cardiff Cymry Cymraeg use the place as a living room. The beer is great too – the scrawl in my notebook says this – but I can't in fact remember. After a passage of time during which drinks arrive and depart we get up to go. Do we? I'm sure we do. It could be last orders or maybe it's Sunday. Behind me lights go off and people leave. I find myself standing in heavy rain at the bottom end of the great ride up Pontcanna Fields to Llandaf. That was it. The Half Way was half way between the city of Cardiff and the city of Llandaf. Brilliant. Can't find my notebook in order to write the revelation down. Will I remember it? Might.

Songs To Sing In Cardiff
When You Are Drunk

Hey, Baby
Wonderwall
Who Let The Dogs Out
Delilah
Sex Bomb I'm your Sex Bomb
You'll Never Walk Alone
Twist & Shout
Hymns and Arias
Sospan Fach
Myfanwy
Calon Lan Mine Lawn Daioni
Here We Go Here We Go
Asda doodah what the hell is it
hum
useless whistle
dum dum

VICTORIA PARK

On Cowbridge Road the Vic is not what it was. They don't dance here
now. The Victoria Ballroom – beat groups, soft drinks, haze of dope
– has closed, It's now *The Victoria Social Club – Weddings, Parties,
Retirement dos, Christenings, Brains*. Upstairs where the dance floor
once was are now offices. Most of them To Let. The road to
Cowbridge here was once the turnpike that crossed Ely Moors –
unlit, undrained, a marshland of trench and tumble. I go up past the
Vic and on to Summers Funeral Home then Edmund's Buildings, a
stubby row of mid-nineteenth century cottages, all kitted with nine-
on-nine replacement Georgian windows. The row is set back from
the road at a slight angle and its cottages have long front gardens.
They don't fit the rest of the Victoria neighbourhood. Relics of what
went before.

Kingsland Road, on the right, was where my father had enthusias-
tically brought us after a deal to live in Marlborough Road had
collapsed. Three stories, cast-iron fireplaces, attic skylights, shaky

Victorian balcony, shed out back. We lived here for less than a year before moving back across the city to the familiar east. The neighbourhood is now demographically mixed. Sari, turban, veil, shopping trolley, badly-fitting running pants. Our brick house is now unevenly clad in imitation sandstone which makes it look like a giant Airfix kit. Opposite someone has stored three illuminated full-sized santas, two snowmen, a plastic reindeer and sleigh the size of a Toyota Yaris on their balcony. Christmas waits.

Kingsland runs parallel to the gem of the district – Victoria Park. It's named after the monarch who was in full jubilee mode at the time of its 1897 opening. The Park is laid on a drained section of Ely Common that according to the 1880 OS Map, originally consisted of pond and swamp. There's a lake at its centre today, empty when I get there in the February cold. In the spirit of water it's painted blue and faces a cabin which sells Coke, Tangos, Slush Puppies and Choc-top Mivy Double-frozen Toffee Feasts. The technicolor display ads stuck to the glass try hard to look like Marbella. The anorexic sales assistant cowers in a back room over a tiny electric fire.

Victoria Park with its MacFarlane Drinking Fountain and Canopy (restored and re-sited 1980), its carefully laid paths, pool, play area, toilets, tennis courts and bowling green is a Cardiff classic. Green, formal, open, dogs, skateboards, bikes. And the district has taken its name to its heart. Victoria Park Wines, Victoria Park Clinic, Victoria Park Mazda, Victoria Park Post Office, the Victoria Park Hotel, Victoria Park Service Station. There's a window-full of splendid For Sales at Graham Allen, all in Victoria Park. But the reality is that this is west

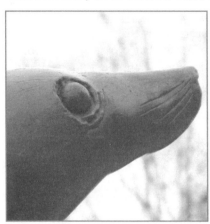

Canton. Check the nearby Canton Liberal Workingmen's Club, The Canton Grapevine, or the Canton Chinese Delight. Like Roath Park in east Cardiff the district is an aspirational middle-class myth. It's an unofficial attempt to outdistance Canton's hoary hands. An estate agent's dream creation. Space and greenery. Victoria Park, Parish of Canton reads a sign. Ely Common says the map. I give up.

Billy the Seal, centrepiece of a great deal of 70s Cardiff nostalgia, was star attraction at the zoo that occupied these gardens between the wars. Amid bantam storks, a few monkeys, guinea-pigs, rabbits, a pole-cat, a wallaby and a pool of carp, Billy played to the crowds. Fished out of the Irish Sea by mistake in 1912 and landed at Cardiff by a Neale 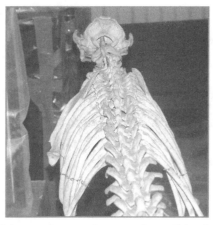 and West trawler the seal starred in many an urban myth until her[8] death in 1939. In the periodic floods that troubled the district when the Ely broke its banks and filled Cowbridge Road with three foot of water Billy is reputed to have regularly escaped. She swam to City Hall, the central fishmarket, the Docks, Roath Park Lake, Thompson's Park fountain, the Severn estuary and up the River Taff. Caught everytime and returned to safety. Fishy Evans, the local hand-cart fishmonger from Telford Street, borrowed Billy to sit among his cod and hake as an advertisement. Between the wars fish were a power in the land. David Petersen has sculpted a life-size seal replica which sits on a rock, north of the pond. Unveiled in 1997 its arrival co-incided almost exactly with NMGW's[9] decision to remove Billy's preserved skeleton from display at Cathays Park and put her in storage. Another myth dispatched. Children are no longer excited by bones. When I ask at the Museum the volunteer part-timer on the information desk tells me that Billy might be at the end of the Natural History Gallery, unless of course that's a shark. It turns out to be a multi-media sea turtle. The real Billy is elsewhere. I get Peter Howlett, Curator of Vertebrates, to prove that the seal has not been sold on for glue. She's on a stand in the corner of the Museum's Globe Works Store at Ocean Way. Head loose, much smaller than I remember, teeth tight together in a lock-jawed smile, bones milky-white and fragile. The store itself is surreal – walls of antelope heads, packing cases marked *Horse* or *Chough* or *Hooded Crow*, lines of plastic-bagged standing birds, head of lioness growling from a black bin-bag, turtles loose across the floor. Billy is next to a model of a

giant microbe. Will she return? Maybe. When the time is right. NMGW obviously underestimate the seal's significance. If Cardiff issued postage stamps Billy would be on them.

Going back to the car from Victoria Park, through the February ice-box, I pass a string of restaurants – Sergio's, Nishirath, Han Sing, Star of India – Barry Edgar Pilcher territory from the time when he had a flat above the Star and let curry seep into everything he owned – his saxophone, his poetry, his mail-art rubber stamps, his felt-pen illuminations of the hippy kingdom. Pilcher, peace, love and saxophones of reality, was the wild man of the 70s Cardiff literary scene. He came at things tangentially. His masterwork was *Magic City*, Cardiff on amphetamine, drizzle and desire, written with Mark Williams and brought out by Speed Limit Publications of Neath. "I want some dope / to take my mind / off not having any". In 1975 I published a pamphlet by him – *Fingers Of Wind* – one of the last gasps from my poetry press, Second Aeon. Pilcher's book was a bunch of stapled sheets done on yellow foolscap and with a sponge of poster paint smeared onto the front as a cover. The run was short but sales were steady. Poetry for the floating. Torrance was a fan. Pilcher was in his slope-pitched cricket team at Llanfairfechan. Out of your head sport in the boiling sun. Pilcher skydiving. Like Ken Kesey, he was destined forever to go Further. "This curry, man, breathe it and you can fly", he'd say through a cloud of poetry dope. Coltrane of the airing cupboard – blowing a storm into the drug heated night. Like Billy not there now. Moved to the far west of Ireland where the air was pure. Had the dream and stayed with it. Star of India, Canton. So ordinary now.

TINKINSWOOD

It's a lot further west to Tinkinswood. The directions for access, posted on the web by the Ramblers, are much more to do with the walking than the getting there. I should have realised this. The car is abandoned in a leafy lay-by on the Old Port Road west of St Lythans. The port is Barry, Cardiff's great coal exporting rival of the nineteenth century. That was when Davies the Ocean[10] tackled Bute head on as a dock builder and a railway operator and, for a time, managed to get more tonnage sailing out of Barry's deeper waters than his rival did from Cardiff. The city won in the end, of course. You can hear it faintly behind us, the distant low thrum of its traffic, the murmuring as it moves, the noise it makes bending the air. But we're far enough out for that not to matter.

A great walk should always contain an element of surprise. Today that turns out to be Duffryn Nurseries, "Specimen and architectural plants", hidden up a lane behind Homefarm, past a corn storage facility and a barn full of silage-covered machinery. This is no conventional garden centre selling plant stakes, gnomes and bedding crysanths. Duffryn Nurseries deal in what's known as the ready garden and feature mature Acer in giant cart-away pots, ten-foot New Zealand tree ferns and entangling thickets of dark bamboo. Do not arrive in your Fiesta and expect your purchases to fit in the back. I am taken by a variegated ornamental grass in a container about the size of an armchair but can't see how I could get it into my rucksack. The nursery barn-cum-warehouse is full of freshly watered fern and

steams in the late-August heat. Burges, Bute's architect, would have sourced plants like these, and in these quantities, for his roof gardens at Cardiff Castle. But this lot are destined for Vale houses where twenty-first century professionals need instant green gratification and the bamboo has become the new fern.

The route on takes us along the south end of the Duffryn

estate and through the outskirts of Dyffryn Village. The lanes are mud dusty, grass overgrown, and slow. The path to Tinkinswood is north, over a stile, through a fence and up the long fields, following a line of electric cable. This is rich Vale farm land, lamb, beef. The ground rises along the line of Thomas Mawson's great 1906 Dyffryn Garden. This sixty-nine acre masterpiece of Italian and Roman terrace, yew-hedged enclosure, rose garden, arboretum and lily pond belongs to the Vale Council and is currently being restored with Lottery cash. The house it surrounds is an ancestral pile going back to pre-Elizabethan times. Its origins, I'm officially told, are in the little-recorded age when King Judhail and Bishop Oudoceous held sway. Remember them? No, neither do I.

I came here first in the sixties when the house was run by Glamorgan County Council as a sort of training and induction centre for staff. I spent a long weekend in the company of fifty or so others being taught how to answer a telephone, when to wear your jacket and how to operate a two-pronged filing punch. The Gardens were a wet alien world. Empty brown ale bottles floated among the lily pads. A new generation of clerks took slow pulls on their Park Drive in the cactus house. Personal handbooks on the importance of local authority services to the local voter lay unopened on our beds.

Later the house became a venue for arts activities which included open-air theatre and indoor literary conferences. Top of the list was the annual summer gathering of the largely blue-rinse SAMWAW, the South and Mid-Wales Association of Writers. SAMWAW loved to look at the paying markets for romantic fiction, thrillers, bodice-ripper serials and articles on caravan dwelling, coarse fishing and financial investment. A favourite was their annual short fiction competition which attracted entries from all over the UK, offered a real prize (contributed by Matthew Pritchard, heir to the Agatha Christie *Mouse Trap* millions) and got won by people with a genuine talent. SAMWAW conferences had a pre-War feel to the way they operated. Committee members wore square badges, delegates sported triangles, those of the chair and former chair were edged in red, panellists had round badges, guest speakers wore oblongs. The bookseller (and I sometimes occupied this position) anarchically wore no badge at all. Gentlemen were asked to bring appropriate formal clothing, ladies were advised to pack a long dress. There was a grand dinner on the Saturday evening. This was followed by an opportunity to go to bed early. There were poets present occasionally but usually they kept pretty quiet. Doesn't happen there now. Prices rose, pensions shrank.

Tinkinswood is a six-thousand year old cairn with a 24 by 15 foot capstone, the largest in Britain. This forty-ton slab of rock would have taken at least two hundred people to lift into place. The official access is by turning off the A48 at St Nicholas, parking on the roadside and using CADW's designated route through a ditch and over two fields. But we're approaching from the south. As we get near the gigantic capstone appears like a prehistoric bunker on the rising ground. Llech-y-Filiast, Maes-y-Filiast. Spirits float through the trees. As a cairn Tinkinswood is about as impressive as they come. A horned forecourt of drystone masonry built in a herringbone pattern leads to a large chamber in which were found a thousand pieces of bone and pot fragment. Dating showed the tomb to have been in use for thousands of years. Sleep here before May Day, say the folk tales, and you'll either die or go mad. Or have to write your way out of the experience in holy verse. The boulders in a ragged line to the south of the cairn are women turned to stone for dancing on the Sabbath. Ancient swords are under the uprights. The Holy Grail lies buried in the fields nearby. The ley energy pours from here to nearby St Lythans on its way south to Arthur's landing place on the Severn shore. The Loyal Arthurian Warband, a tribe of hippies, anarchists and other fellow travellers, use the site to knight their followers. Bodily fluids are expelled and exchanged. In their robes and bearing shields, swords, and amulets, they come here after dark has fallen. Moon shadow. Light leaking around the capstone edges. They are ragged new age believers, priests, druids. Although not one, as far as I can tell, is from that other gathering of druids – Gorsedd Beirdd Ynys Prydain, the Welsh Gorsedd of the Bards. Tinkinswood's ancient name is Castell Corrig, the Castle of the Dwarfs, of the diminutives who occupied Wales before the giants came. Giants Grave, Giants Grove, Giants Road, Giants Step, Giants Walk, Giants Causeway. Who were they, these giants? Us I suppose. We're all bigger now, just have a look at the height of old church doorways or the effigies of saints and ancient worthies in medieval repose.

What you get out of Tinkinswood depends on your background. It's a peaceful place, green, well cared-for. Something of the ancients still hangs onto it despite the excavation brick capstone-support inside, put there by Edwardian archaeologists. It's unobtrusive enough, weathered by now, visible only when you peer inside. Present-day safety experts would no doubt advise blue high-visibility handrails and a complete absence of strangulation points. There's a family climbing over it when we arrive. An eight-year old with a toy gun shoots at imaginary invaders. Inside are the ash ends of a burned joss stick, candle wax and the remains of a fire. Ritual still circles. Sun through the trees. The path back to the car lies beyond.

COSMESTON

Mami Ando and I are on the culture trail. Cardiff has put art in the parks and we're looking. Mami is here from Abiko City, Japan, where the bullet train does 300 miles an hour taking people to work and a melon costs $100. She's in Wales seeking rural quaintness but she doesn't call it that. We drive to the park through the brand new Bute Tunnel, black tarmac, lights, escape hatches, James Bond, and Mami doesn't bat an eyelid. I tell her the story about the excavators getting to within three feet of the Packet's beer cellar as they drilled through. She looks at me blankly. Urban aggrandisement is too universal. But Cosmeston with sun, water, nature and art is different. Real, bright, usable. All we know is that the art is somewhere in the woods and the site is over 100 hectares. Could be anywhere.

Cosmeston is a country park built on a reclaimed limestone quarry. A greenfield brownfield site, as it were. The quarry, which was worked

from the 1890s to the 1960s, supplied stone for Penarth's Ferrocrete cement works. When Ferrocrete closed excavation ceased and the empty pits slowly filled with water. The name *Cosmeston* is a corruption of *Costinston*, which was "one of the manors granted by King Edward VI to Sir William Herbert[11]." No doubt the title, Lord of Cosmeston Manor, has been sold on to an American or a Yorkshire businessman by now. In 1978 the Council discovered the collapsed walls of a manor house and other medieval foundations just south of the lakes. These have been developed into a sort of actors-in-costume St Fagans embellished with rare pig breeds. As we pass there's a sign advertising a day of diversions which includes MEDIEVAL MAYHEM! all

pointedly exclamationed. It's a punctuation people use when they run out of real words, I tell Mami, but she's not interested. Grammar can come later.

The Park is an undoubted success. Wood-slatted walkways, ponds, picnic areas, reed beds, nature trails, discrete interpretative notice boards. The wildlife is extensive – Tufted Duck, Dab, Heron, flocks of Mute Swan with cygnets in tow, Great Crested Grebe, diving Coot, Goldfinch – with plenty of fenced off conservation areas along with signs warning of dire consequence if you cross the barrier without a permit. According to the leaflet that we've picked up from the interpretation centre there are Purple Loosestrife, Greater Spearwort, Pyramidal Orchid, Green Woodpecker, and Oxeye Daisy in the paddock we are passing. The ground rises slowly, quarry slurry recolonised, Elm and Hawthorn thickening, and that hot buzz of insects that only occurs when the air is still.

The art work is elusive. It's called *Carpet* something. We've lost the exhibition guide. We do the hunt from memory. Mami decides it can't be on the main trail and has to be deeper in the woods. We follow a rough, much smaller path in between overhanging oak and ash. There are bird hides here, made of wood, greening into the background. Some of them have broken doors. We spot fragments of vandalised roof strewn among the bushes. Someone has built a rope swing across a clearing. Bright blue yacht line trails above a mud flattened gash. In the undergrowth are crushed drink cans, rusted railings, collapsed fruit boxes, a car seat. Is this it, asks Mami? Trash in twilight. We are standing on a stretch of Royal Red Axminster laid between the trees.

It has a scroll pattern around its edge. Trunk and bush rise through holes cut for the purpose. The wool follows the ground's contour. *Carpet.* Is this it? Art at last. Yes. Or maybe no. I rub my hand across the woven surface. It's wet.

On the way out, strolling past the Eastern Lake, we encounter an extended Asian family. They enter with wheeled barbeque, curry pots, saucepans, cool boxes, grandma with hair died orange in a wheelchair, five kids with bikes and scooters, overweight sons lugging bags containing cutlery, chapatti and drink and then a father in a white shirt and beaming face, sweating, shouldering a rug to lie on. In Cardiff carpets are certainly part of the culture. Mami nods her head.

ST LYTHANS

The dual carriageway leading out from the city rises at speed towards the Vale. This is Cowbridge Road West, the dividing line between Ely and Caerau. It passes the infamous Dusty Forge and the remains of the great Avenue Cinema, once a Rolls & Bentley main dealer and now, keeping the spirit, Blockbuster Video. The speed limit on the highway switches from 30 to 40, almost in secret. Patrol cars prowl amid the mix of souped Ford Escorts and battered Golfs. Speed cameras leer from their stubby poles. If it were not for the shell-suits and combat trousers drinking from bright yellow glasses outside the Culverhouse this could be Florida. The sky blues up above the dual roundabouts at Culverhouse Cross. This is a city peripheral retail park: Marks & Spencer, Tesco, Homebase, Powerhouse, PC World, car parks, trolleys. HTV studios beyond them. This was a Vale farm once, now encroached by expanding Cardiff. The Culver House was a shack where they kept pigeons and doves, opposite the cemetery. Long gone.

The way to St Lythans is through Wenvoe, a Vale of Glamorgan village not yet Cardiff but might as well be. Wenvoe, Gwenfo in Welsh, Gwaynvo according to Iolo Morganwg, the great eighteenth century faker of Welsh History. According to Iolo in "about 1046" the Norman "Sir Robert Fitz Haymon" gave Wenvoe to one of his knights, Sir John Flemming, who built a strong castle here. I get this from a transcript in the *Cardiff Records.* My copy comes to me bought as surplus from the library of Howell's Girls School. There's a neat pencilled note in the margin which reads "This account is full of errors. It is of no authority at all." A bit like Iolo himself, really. There's no sign of the castle when I get there. Day now like an oven. You mean the pub, suggests a local, dog, hat, leaning on a stick. I don't.

Parked, I head north across rising ground, through dense wood to emerge on the edge of the Wenvoe Castle Golf Club. I'm heading for the St Lythans Neolithic chambered cairn. This is county not city. Horse boxes. Bridleways. Families in paddocks messing with saddlery. Feed. Four-wheelers. The Castle, I discover, is now the golf clubhouse, Robert Adam's eighteenth century manor house with castellations, most of it destroyed by fire in 1910[12]. The path goes up the east side of the fairway, way-marked. Despite the heat golfers are still in their yellow Pringle sweaters. They pointedly ignore me. Wrong clothes. Wrong shoes. Vibram sole 14-eyelet boots don't make it here. I cross east through shoulder tall bracken, bramble-edged, nettle, dock, and climb long fields dragging my feet through calf-high grass. From the brow of the hill the megalith appears in startling isolation. Green on all sides. Paths do not lead to it. Nothing is built near. Looking back from this spot the whole of west Cardiff from the Barrage to St Fagans lies spread. Greenery covering the quarry edges, traffic glinting in the steaming sun.

St Lythans village is a cluster of houses, Ravenswood Farm, St Lythans Church with its Saxon boundary wall and button chapel. For the product of a race of small people the cairn is spectacularly tall. These burial chambers were built in the 4th millennium BC, three uprights topped with a huge capstone, not as big as Tinkinswood but still impressive. The bodies went inside, the whole structure was covered with earth. What we see now is the skeleton, the tomb girders, the unholy innards as they were never expected to be viewed. Rolling centuries of looters, gold seekers, marauders, thieves and vandals have seen the chamber stripped of its outriders, its covering and all its content. I can walk right into the revealed chamber without bending. This is Maesyfelin, Mill Field. Last century it was used as a shelter for animals. Outlying stones were stolen for farmer's walls

What's amazing about St Lythans, apart from its size and state of almost immaculate preservation, is how near this is to the big city and how, apparently, little visited. I am here on a Sunday afternoon in high season and there's no one else about. I paw the grass looking for traces: dropped druidic amulets, fragments of helmet, bits of ancient sword. But all I find is a can ring-pull. Same thing.

Back at the Wenvoe Castle, the pub not the golf club, the clientele appear to consist entirely of youth, souped-Peugeot and cider. Eminen. Tupac. Jay-Z. What's Wenvoe famous for, I ask someone with a Beckham haircut. Nothing, he says, picking lint from his jeans, head nodding to the rap from outside. Cardiff's mystic periphery. The St Lythans capstone spins.

notes

1. *Environs of Cardiff 1840* as re-drawn by John Hobson Matthews
2. In Welsh *Pont* means Bridge
3. Pont Canna – The northern part of the hamlet of Canton (1702.) The bridge from which it takes its name was probably the little rude stone one which here crossed the Whitehouse Brook. Both bridge and brook disappeared in 1896, with the old Pontcanna Cottages hard by, when the northern portion of Cathedral Road was completed" (Cardiff Records, 1898). The bridge itself was little more than a couple of slabs slung across the Canna's ditch.
4. Pontcanna Cottages show up clearly on both the Tithe maps from the 1840s and the OS's detailed survey of the 1880s.
5. The Whitehouse Bridge 'in a place called Durton' or Turton (Plas-Turton), near the site known as King's Castle" – *Cardiff, A History of the City*, Corporation of the City of Cardiff, 1969
6. The Whitehouse ditch was condemned as a nuisance and filled in during 1874. Some traces remained until 1895. When it flowed this rivulet was reputed to mark the ancient boundary between the parishes of Cardiff and Llandaf.
7. James Hawes
8. Despite the name Billy turned out to be female
9. NMGW – National Museums and Galleries of Wales
10. David Davies, Llandinam 1818-1890
11. Matthews – Cardiff Records
12. Robert Adam built the manor house in 1776 for the industrialist Peter Birt on the site of an earlier medieval castle. The style was Roman fortress with a castellated roof. Only the east flank now remains. Wenvoe Golf Club took over the site – house, grounds, stables, grotto and serpentine canal in 1936.

NORTH

THE POOL AT MAINDY

There are afternoons when the rain in this city does not press. This is one. Top of my shoulders warm. Light in the usually overcast sky. I've come up from the civic centre in search of Jack Crabtree's Maindy Pool. This painting[1], which has somewhat prophetically in its foreground a small self-portrait face wearing old-fashioned swim goggles, hangs in the National Museum. It depicts Maindee as a green effluent swirl surrounded by houses, trees and urban waste. But in the real world that pool is long gone. It was here in the nineteenth century when Maindy was a clay pit – a sump from which daub and then brick had been dug – filled with sixty-five foot of water, sprung up from the swamp of Cardiff, driven there by our unending rain. Between the wars the pool was drained as the city built itself a stadium and cycle track. It was walled using building stone rescued from the nearby and recently abandoned Glamorgan Canal. As a district at that time Maindy was industrial – coach works, engine repair, paint – smoke and dust. Don Skene cycled to victory around Maindy's sloping track. Watching crowds in caps and waistcoats sucked on their Woodbines. The working man relaxed.

The Stadium today has been redeveloped. The red cycle track has been widened. The pool has been put back as a Cardiff Council sports and leisure facility. No effluent but a sting of chlorine. There are green plantings and a savagely angled car park. I get there walking up past the North Road BP Garage, Kwik-Fit Exhausts (open Sundays, everything guaranteed) and the Kingdom Hall of Jehovah's Witnesses

(meeting times advertised on a peg board plus a reassurance to visitors that demands for money will not be made). Kingdom Hall was black and distinctive corrugated iron for decades. Its replacement is undistinguished red brick. The Stadium is opposite, spread between Crown Way Companies House and Cardiff's Maindy Army Barracks. The Royal Regiment of Wales Head Quarters have been here since 1871 when they moved up from the Longcross[2]. They hide behind trees, wrapped in wire, leaf screened into invisibility. No threat. The peace protesters don't see them. No one chains themselves to these anonymous gates.

The track centre has been marked as a soccer pitch. Mown grass. Gone are the running tracks. I went round

those in my schooldays. There's a photo of me doing it. I look like Roger Bannister. Sweatless. White vest. Bones. Cliff Richard hair. I lean on the rail and watch the past. It's in mono. Adam Faith is singing 'What Do You Want…' I've black daps on my feet and brightness in my eyes.

Today the Stadium is full of kids on small bikes, fathers on their mobiles and mothers with pushchairs the size of wheelbarrows. Sunday. Two men with shaved heads, one with a Robbie Williams bicep tattoo, the other with a roll-up, stand beside the open boot of a Vectra discussing football. Lil Kim thrums from someone's speakers. There is no blowing litter. No graffiti. No one I can see has a Heineken in his hand. Small town safe. Crabtree's detritus has been vanquished. Here at least.

LLYS TAL Y BONT

The main road through Maindy crosses the old Taff Vale main line and heads north as a dual carriageway fronted by Cathays High School. In the sixties this was the hotbed of one of Welsh lit's early flowerings when Geraint Jarman banged out pre-Alfred Street verse in English and D A Callard was his acolyte. At that time Wales meant something, for a long time after didn't, but now does again. Fickle cycle. What goes around comes around. Today there are pubs in Cardiff named after Free Wales Army bombers (see page 97 – The

Cayo Arms). In the sixties his army-surplus-clad irregulars marched on Llandaf Fields. Fellow-travellers had rounds bought for them in the Conway. Jarman was a fan. Said he was. Not now. In 1969 in The New Ely someone showed me a set of knuckle dusters. Metal things like stair rod clips. Said he was going to Caernarfon to help sort things out. Need to raise the cash for the fare. I gave him half a crown.

Opposite the Porsche Garage, next to the old weighbridge now restyled as Nice'N'Tasty Burgers (closed), Parkfield Place runs at right angles down to the river. This is working class Cardiff from the first great mid-nineteenth century boom. Here were once Patent Fuel Works, Wagon Builders, the Crown, the Star and Anchor factories. Sheds where men cut metal, sliced timber, pressed coal dust into pitch to make burnable briquettes. Caps, collarless shirts, arms and faces black as miners. Two up, two down, street facing terraces, tin bath on a hook out back. Today it's all university accommodation. Student lets, houses with sinks full of unwashed plates and rivers of lager can flowing down the halls.

As it drops through this rich cultural mix Parkfield Place becomes Llys Talybont Road falling towards the line of the old Glamorgan Canal, the tarmaced Taff Trail and the dark river itself. In this place once stood one of Glamorgan's oldest mansions – Llys Tal y Bont, *The Court at the Head of the Bridge* – no crossing now, the bridge gone. Llystalybont is a magic name in Welsh history. In our wet country where nothing lasts this place goes back to the early dawn. Home of Ifor Bach. Court of the chieftains who followed him. Seat of the Welsh princes from the Roman period right up to the feudal.

Power centre for a swath of land that ran from Soudrey in the south to Whitchurch, Llanishen and Lisvane up north.

As a place of significance Talybont had rights. It had its own monastery at Mynachdy. The Lord was entitled to receive waifs, estrays, goods of felons, deodands, treasure trove, escheats, fines, forfeitures, amercements, and perquisites of court, double rent on death or alienation, avowries, suits of mill from copyholders and a penny per head for any cattle impounded. It's all listed in the scrolls. The power of ancient bureaucracy backed, naturally, by ancient sword.

In the Welsh way of things this was no great Elizabethan house, of course, for the building pre-dated that English monarch. It was instead a short row of cottages – stable attached, converted, incorporated. Photographs show the building still standing, thatched, as late as 1901. When I get there the path in has a new name – Bevan Way – and the site is surrounded by concrete student flats and a pressed metal quick-build sports centre. Oak and plane tree soften the contemporary intrusion. Llys Tal y Bont is still here, at least a version of it is. Re-roofed, new stack, new pots, new windows, new sills, new frames, new doors, lean-to demolished, walls rendered inside and out, white painted, floors replaced, carpets put down. Powell Duffryn used the place as a pay office in the fifties, Manpower Services had it in the seventies. In 1984 a Cardiff City Council community programme "upgraded" it. There's a small red plaque on the wall which tells us so. The past has been smoothed off, layer by layer, until nothing remains. It's a training centre now. The manager, intrigued as to why I'm photographing it, shows me around. Anything old left? No. But the walls are thick. 18" to two foot. They've got to be ancient, he tells me. No walls are that thick today. And Oliver Cromwell slept here. Cromwell certainly got around.

Up the Taff Trail beyond stands one of Burges' adornments of the Bute Estate, the Park Keeper's lodge, now converted to private use. Nineteenth century looking so much older than Llys Tal y Bont. History once more wiped. We do this so often, so thoroughly, so well.

GABALFA

If you look on the early twentieth century maps of Cardiff, Gabalfa is little more than a stretch of fields and a house by the side of the Taff. *Gabalfa*, a corruption of the Welsh *ceubalfa*, means *place of the ferry*. It fits. Llandaff Cathedral is on the far western side of the river. Worshippers from east Cardiff would have needed to get there somehow. But the ferry house is no more. Gabalfa Primary School now stands on the spot. The Gabalfa Estate, largely a post-war construction, now occupies the flood plain set in the vee between the Taff and its tributary, Nant-Gwaedlyd, the Whitchurch Brook[3]. These were allotments, piggeries, smallholdings before the houses came. The estate is compact with a population of around eight and half thousand. Not known for violence, drugs at a minimum, trees rarely set on fire, no stoning of buses. The Glamorgan Canal (see page 130) used to run through the centre along the line of the estate's grand boulevard, Gabalfa Avenue. This is a fine example of one of the great distinguishing marks of council development – sweeping roadways with grass-filled central reservations and grass borders that separate pavement from tarmac. Effortlessly they pull the eye down along their regal grandness. But rather than Mercs parked outside mock Georgian detached you get Fiestas with speed stripes parked four-wheels full on the pavement and rapid-construct brick semis, some with applied stick-on stone finish, others with front lawns worn flat by dogs, kids and junk.

I'm here looking for the last of the Cardiff prefabs, the 1940s instant housing erected on bomb sites and meant to last for fifteen years. Winston Churchill wanted housing that was quick, erectable by the unskilled and manufacturable by new processes using new materials.

The *Arcon* was made from asbestos sheets, the *Taran* and the *Uni-Seco* incorporated pressed concrete on a timber frame, the *Aluminium* used the metal from surplus aircraft. In all 4,300 went up across bomb blasted south Wales. Newport got the *Arcon*, Cardiff the *Aluminium*. These futuristic bungalows were streets ahead of their time. They had built in kitchens, central services, ducted warm-air heating and copious amounts of cupboard space. They came off the production line at the rate of one every twelve minutes. They were shipped complete on the backs of lorries. Once the foundations were made they could be erected in a couple of hours. The Cardiff

examples are in Llandinam Crescent and Boncath Road.

I cycle in because on a bike you are invisible. Cars are too fast and you have to park them. On foot and you are an intruder, a visitor with a purpose, someone to be watched. On a bike you sail silent, en route to somewhere else. You can look at the world but the world rarely looks back. Half way up Aberporth Road I ask someone cutting his hedge where the metal bungalows might be. "Gone, mate. You're a year too late. They've got real houses now." And they have: fresh bungalows, new brick, double glazed, garden centre planted fronts, roofs that don't leak. The one prefab that's been preserved – a Type B2 Aluminium from Llandinam Crescent – has been transported a few miles west to St Fagans. It sits there, opposite Llanrwst's Hendre-wen barn, kitted out with 1950s plywood utility furniture, *Woman's Own* on the bed, hats on the hook in the hall. Visitors are often those who used to actually live there, or in something pretty similar. There's a family going through in front of me with the grandmother loudly telling the world that her bedspread was just like the one the Museum's got and that these places were cold and damp in the winter but if she hadn't had to she wouldn't have changed a thing. For decades the Council adopted the same approach. Fifteen year temporary dwellings were made to last for fifty. And when officialdom at last decided to pull them down the residents formed action committees in an attempt to stay the Council's hand.

At the top end of the estate past the Gabalfa Avenue shops – Spar, Video Express, Hardware, *No Dogs In Shop*, Hairdressers (closed), the Master Gunner, Londis with *wankers* spray-painted across its frontage, broken down fast food van *Good food Hot Snacks Breakfast Rolls Burgers* stuck in someone's front garden, I find the Gabalfa Avenue Day Centre. There are metal shutters across all doors and windows, armoured grills, and spiked fence along the roof rim, no lamps armoured or otherwise anywhere. It's like Belfast. But so silent. This is Sunday and it's hot. There was once a humped-back canal bridge here and a pub called the Three Cups. Both gone. At St Marks, on the edge of Llandaff North, there's a dog show in progress in the churchyard. At the TA Centre someone's fixing a new wheel onto a rusting auto. There are no army vehicles visible. No one is in uniform. Maybe it's not like Belfast after all.

To the west of the Gabalfa estate, rising up the edge of what would have been the Taff Valley, lies Mynachdy[4], still council, hard to tell where one district ends and the next begins. The locals don't know either. On Cefn Road a pensioner cleaning his car tells me that this is Birchgrove. A man with a beard and a dog calls it the Philog. On Radyr Place a youth on a bike tells me that Mynachdy is the other side of the motorway. The smiling Bangladeshi walking up Mynachdy Road itself apologises for having no idea. Does Gabalfa actually exist? Yet again, everyone seems to want to be somewhere else. The schizophrenia of the street names doesn't help. Appledore Road, Lydstep Flats[5], Aberteifi Crescent, Llanmorlais Road. But maybe that's the purpose. Cardiff – capital of Anglo-Wales. No one round here seems to have named their home *Cartref*, not yet.

I exit through the complex of paths and pedestrian underpasses that surround the A470 / Western Avenue interchange. The pillars are well graffitied. *Ribena Funds Animal Torture, Darren loves (unintelligible)*, and then in two-foot letters on the side of descending steps that singular name: *Lord Bute*. Still around after all these years, then. It's a great tag.

HEOL Y WAUN

The moon gazing was a failure. Too much cloud filling the night sky. Sheet grey. Cold. Bashō. Zen. Becoming. Matsuo Bashō, 1644-94, haiku master, did not live in post-industrial south Wales. He came from Edo[6], pre-industrial, lantern-lit, Japan. I've come in from the garden at Heol y Waun, Whitchurch, Cardiff, where I've built a bamboo rail. String-strapped poles under the cherry tree, chrysanthemums in the border. Lean on it in your kimono if you have one. Moon up there somewhere glowering. Couldn't see it at all.

Bashō aspired to a life that was continuous and deep. The one we had was neither. He wanted to give every action, every moment all the value that it potentially had. This life would become the greater life. Every flower would be the spring. Every wave the ocean. Every scratch of light the entire heavens. He moon gazed. Took boats to sea for a better view. Leant on the rail he'd erected at the foot of his garden, between the plum and the bamboo, stared at the sky. Moon. Light. The bright singularity. No need for words. I'm Bashō, twentieth century, I'd like to be. A haiku poet who doesn't count his syllables, omits the seasons, leaves himself in everything. Gaze but do not stick. I cannot yet detach myself. One side of the rail sunk in the lawn clay, the fixing on the other coming slowly undone.

In Cardiff there's antipathy. The form is entirely misunderstood. Strict meter Welsh poets deride it because it lacks internal structure, goes no where, hangs so simply just where it is. "On the sandy beach, Footprints: Long is the spring day." (Shiki). No skill in this. Self-effacing. Empty. Welsh verse demands vocabulary, history, rhythm, engagement, passion, delight. But the haiku is so different. Empty but for the hint of an echo. Essence. A grasping at the inexpressible. Meaning beyond meaning. The sound of one hand clapping. The face you had before you were born. Nothing. Everything. Zen.

Do not hunt in here for the crisp clip of meaning. It is not available. Understand by understanding, not by working it out. The geese do not wish to leave their reflection behind; the water has no mind to retain their image. Somewhere here lies poetry. Wait for it to arrive.

Bashō has this haiku about a pond and a frog. Famous, but awkward in garrulous English: The frog stands on the rock. / Jumps into the pond below. / Surface breaks with a sonorous clap. In the Japanese the syllables are so short – one letter, two at most. In English they sprawl out, three letters, four, five. The verse lumbers. Dom Sylvester Houedard, concrete poet, monk at Prinknash Abbey, experimenter with typograms, mirror verse, poetry of single words, has sent his version. Felt pen on transparent paper. It hangs on the study wall.

Frog   Pond   Plop

Three word zip. More Bashō than Sylvester. Reduced to the essence. The very sound changing as the word dips into the reader's consciousness, sinks below. Becomes. Bashō dead three hundred years. dsh just taking off[7].

Like the bamboo rail I tried to build in my garden my first haiku, written at the height of the sixties, failed on all counts:

Look at the sky
He shouted
Staring up her skirt[8].

Bashö was the name on the spine of a book I had yet to read. The
Narrow Road to the Deep North led to Merthyr. Cardiff was filled
with the Anglo-Welsh in their second flowering. Frivolity had no
place. Verse was serious business. But the woman from the Arts
Council thought the poem so funny that I didn't care. Try to become
but if you don't then move on.

On the study floor are a clutch of haiku magazines, American,
printed on fine paper, seeds and stalks embedded in the sheet. Single
poem per page. White space in large abundance. Silence surrounding
the verses. I contrast this with my copy of Ken Gearing's *Breakthru*
magazine, cyclostyled, foolscap paper, spine stapled and already
rusting slightly. Sixteen poems to a two page spread, sardines. To get
your stuff considered here you had to subscribe. Pay money. I'd sent
my postal order but my stuff was still not inside.

Glyn Jones had invited me round to look at his collection of literary
magazines. I'd been before. Glyn's pre-War amassment of new lit had
a way of putting today's less well-printed and far too numerous
counterparts into perspective. *Life and Letters Today. Wales. Dublin
Review. Welsh Outlook. The Welsh Review*. Poetry. No haiku. Glyn lived
on Manor Way in a post-War semi that was later to get one of the first
of the Rhys Davies Trust's celebratory plaques hung on its side. Home
of one of Wales' greatest twentieth century English-language poets.
Gone now into the dust of Cardiff history. All that's left is the plaque.

I'm early. I leave Heol y Waun and its clutch of metal window
framed mini-semis – in our front room a six foot man could touch
both walls – and walk up onto College Road. South is the rail bridge,
The Crown, and the northern reaches of the Gabalfa housing estate.
North is the common (the Waun) – the old village and beyond it
Northern Avenue – Manor Way – the A470, dual carriage way
overload.

Do you write haiku, Glyn? He doesn't. Englynion, maybe. They're
the same sort of thing aren't they? Yes, I tell him. Then I correct
myself. No. He holds tea, sups. In later life, right arm amputated,

signing his name in shaky biro with an uncertain left, time for everyone, nicest man alive. I sense the Welsh past just below Glyn's
English surface. We watch the traffic 40 mph smog-thick crawl into
the anglicised city.

Back at Heol y Waun I re-read Bashō[9]. The Glyn Jones of Edo,
with his detachment and his modesty and his drunken friends.

A white chrysanthemum –
However intently I gaze:
Not a speck of dust.

CREIGIAU

Leaving Cardiff for Llantrisant you rise up from the delta into the
South Wales coalfield. Cardiff at last touching that which made it
great. In its most recent expansion (1996) the city took in the villages
of Capel Llanilltern, Pentyrch and Creigiau. Upland parishes. Rising
roadways. Land and hills and far less sky. I'm on the A4119 which
heads for Llantrisant. I've already crossed the edge of urbanisation,
past Cardiff's last thatched cottage[10] (The Thatch at Radyr) and
travel between empty fields. Hedgerows, long grass. 59% OF THE
PUBLIC SAY KEEP HUNTING. Union Jack on a tree. Cardiff's
edge is out beyond here, ready for the next enlargement. Early
clusters of up-market Barrett brick and gable mark the way.

At the far edge, nestling against a stream, the Nant Cessair[11], after
which The Caesar's Arms was named, lies the village of Creigiau.
Creigiau – rocks, crags, a place of stones. The district is almost all
new build middle-class and Welsher than anywhere else in the city –
except possibly parts of Pentyrch and almost certainly Pontcanna.

Morgan and I have driven here from Penarth where we had lunch
at Cafiero Cioni's Bistro and Pizzeria Restaurant on the cliff top. Egg,
beans and chips. I wanted a steak and kidney but they didn't have any.
Morgan claimed, amazingly, never to have eaten pie. Afraid of the
dark meat. So what did you have from your Onllwyn working men's
chippie? Rissole. Morgan is a carpenter from Pant-y-Ffordd, in the
Neath valley, half way between Seven Sisters and Onllwyn, not in the
guidebooks. He's a teacher and a writer – man of hard hands, heart of

gold. With me for the history.

We drive through increasing mist and face-clogging drizzle. We're looking for the Cae-Yr-Arfau cromlech. A ancient burial chamber. CADW listed but to me so far utterly invisible. Morgan also claims not to know what a cromlech is, but I don't believe him. On the map it's shown in a field and the local histories talk of it being bisected by a farm wall, of its capstone sinking, of it being buggered by time, stones stolen, status ignored. Maybe it's no longer there. Wiped out, land ploughed.

In the paddock where it isn't, just beyond the golf club, there are horses, mud and great bales of hay. A stubby public right of way sneaks in here, hits a barbed-wire fence and stops dead. Used to go somewhere, no longer. A mound which Morgan thinks might be ancient is just bramble topping rubble. The cromlech is actually inside the garden of Cae-Yr-Arfau house next door, a gated new-build on the site of an older farm, smart driveway, neat lawns. This is the outer edge of the city. End. Cardiff finishing. The streams seep into the soil. Ditches fill. There was an ancient battle here. Blood on the grass. But, today, just damp.

The cromlech is half covered with stonecrop, ivy and hogweed. When the farmhouse stood this Neolithic home for the dead was distempered white and used as a store for coal. Milk churns stood on the path alongside it. Where the capstone now rests on the boundary wall I can still see a dab of weathered white. Sandra Coslett, the owner, tells me that she may well build a replica of the cromlech on the right side of the house drive. A garden feature. For balance. Much better than a fountain. Does she ever feel disturbed by having new stone age ghosts outside her window? No.

Creigiau's industrial centre was always its quarry. Opened in the 1870s this dolomite pit provided first the stone for the building of Cardiff Docks and later the limestone and magnesium dolomite needed for making steel at Guest-Keen's Tremorfa works. Two trains a day carried rock down the now abandoned mineral line to East

Moors. In the woods the old passenger platform is still there serving an overgrowth of grass tussock, ivy and dogwood. The quarry did small-time road stone and material for river revetments until 2001 when costs outstripped prices and work ceased. The stone crushers were silenced. You could hear the birds again. The largest employer in the district, according the council statistics, became the white painted Caesar's Arms – Hancock's beer, bajan fish cakes, crispy laver balls, tiger prawns in garlic, scallops with leeks and bacon, monkfish, steak.

We look next through the driving mist for Castell y Mynach, medieval farmhouse, the largest in the county. The pub of the same name at Groesfaen is not it. Repaired and repainted the real house, once more residential, is now surrounded on all sides by the rambling Castell y Mynach estate. New paving where the mud tracks were. Stone barns now apartments. Houses in a weave of traffic calming bends, roads that go nowhere, turning circles. Grassed communal space, an urban resolution to the problem of fields. Ffordd Dinefwr twists through the centre. The new dwellings don't shout. Their style blends. The farm has no space to breathe but it's still there. No characterless extensions. No dormer windows. As was, almost. Bricked in gate arches, trefoil-headed lancets. Inside a mighty chimneybreast, shields, medieval paintings on the walls.

In finer weather I'd been here walking and taken the path up beyond the quarry towards Pentyrch hunting for medieval Bristol Fach – *Brysta Fach* – an isolated thatched farm cottage used as a storehouse for saddle leather lugged there from Bristol. The path went up through paddock and field climbing to almost 600 feet and ending at a gash of rubble overgrown with bramble. The cottage had been demolished in the 1980s. For no good reason that I could see. Nothing done with the space. Nothing rebuilt. From here Creigiau looked so totally detached from the city as to be no part of it. I walked back down, through woodland, across the old Craig y Parc estate, passed Pentwyn Farm (that place name again, Pentwyn, the most common in Wales), skirted the iron-age encampment on the hilltop, went along bracken lined bridleways and returned through the forestry along Nant y Glaswg to where I'd begun. Still Cardiff. Cardiff when I started and Cardiff when I was done. Strangest city I'd ever walked through. There's hope yet.

THE GREEN WEDGE

Above the Lake but below Rhydypenau crossroads lies the pond of St Dennis, Llandennis Oval, Ffynnon Dennis, a holy well. This is the start of the Green Wedge, a line of parkland, common land, woodland and open space which runs north along the Lleici river corridor to the Cefn Onn ridge above the city. Dennis was once sixth century Dionysius – (Dionysius – the Latin for Isan) – follower of St Teilo. Monk. Builder of Llans. Llanisan. Llandionysius. Llanishen. Llandennis. You can do a lot with names.

The trail here runs through woods, damp stream crossed remnants of the forests that once filled these lands. They're a thin sliver, squeezed by housing from both sides of Rhyd-y-Penau Road. The Paddock. Woods Covert. Rhydypenau Woods. Oak, beech, alder. Reed beds. Drainage channels. Grey squirrel. Terrier. Collie. Mongrel. Two hundred years ago there were clay pits where the library is, a brick works at the back of Dyffryn Close, and farms: Fid-Las, Rhyd-y-Penau, Rhyd-y-Bilwg, Rhyd-y-Blewyn, Celyn. Today only Rhyd-y-Blewyn remains, house re-roofed, walls rendered, back of Blackoak Road.

The Green Wedge is one of Cardiff's secrets. Or was. Now RAG, the Reservoir Action Group, has arrived, and everyone knows where it is. The southern end, the Nant Fawr Woodlands, are maintained by a community group and used by locals as a short cut – parents with pushchairs, men with dogs, girls with bikes, boys with muddy shoes. In the long summers men in shorts bearing rakes and spades come here

to clear paths and scrape out the bottoms of ponds. The undergrowth is trimmed back. Wild life protected. Nuthatch and woodpecker allowed to flourish.

As it goes north the Wedge hits the twin city reservoirs – Lisvane, built in 1869 to supply Cardiff's booming population, and Llanishen, built a few years later to supply Cardiff's industry and Bute's docks. The Nant Fawr, the Lleici, which runs through their space, helps fill them. Lisvane and Llanishen – 60 acres – interlocked like machine parts. In the early years of the Victorian water industry the countryside around reservoirs – the gathering lands – were closed to the public for fear that the common people would pollute them. At Lisvane and Llanishen public access was discouraged. Strangers with dirt on their boots and disease in their waters might poison the city. Never happened. Although in the sixties, psychedelic anarchists did once try to loose half a jar of lysergic into the waters. Failed. Too stoned to find the way in.

Slowly leisure use increased. First walking, then sailing, then nature rambles, bird watching, looking for fauna and standing stones. But you needed a permit. A couple of pounds a season for walkers, purchasable from resident Welsh Water Rangers. A man smoking a pipe would hail you heartily, ask how you were, and then demand you fill in a form and give him money. Kept the crowds back. Llanishen developed a world reputation as a sailing club. Fly fishermen lined the banks. Bird platforms were built to observe life on Lisvane. Tufted duck. Grebe. Cormorant. Swift. Swallow.

Naturalists discovered waxcap fungi said to be unique to Llanishen. Preservation orders were sought and won. This was biodiversity worth holding onto. Llanishen, Lisvane and the Green Wedge were a resource of the first order.

The path to the reservoirs rises slowly through damp woodland to cross a small, rough car park and enters Welsh Water's land through an iron gate – Cronfa Ddŵr Llanisien – Permit Holders Only – and then your breath gets taken away. Same in the seventies when I came here with the sound poet Bob Cobbing who wanted to see Wales and liked Llanishen's name on the map. We stood there, then, looking at the great expanse of flat, still water stretching out before us. Slate grey like the sky. A swooping cormorant. A diving coot. A row boat at anchor, shrouded in winter canvas. Few buildings. A white-painted keepers house to the left. Hedge. Victorian stone retaining walls. The hills of Cefn Onn rising in the far distance. Woodland below them. Cobbing filled his lungs but made no sounds. Stood there, stunned. Same today, thirty years on. Someone's torched the fishermen's HQ, white with burn marks, part boarded up. Beyond that nothing has changed.

Then it comes on you. The anger. All this is due for development. How can distant owners demand that this space be forsaken in the name of profit? Their company, the U.S. owned Western Power

Distribution (WPD)[12], which now has rights in these acres, has far-reaching designs on their peacefulness. They intend to remove it. Drain the ponds, insert roads, build hundreds of houses, sell them on. Cardiff Council's Unitary Development Plan requires the construction, over the next five years, of new homes for 10,000 people in north east Cardiff. WPD's plans are a gift. On their web site WPD have a map showing their take on the future. Water, reduced by 75%, prominently labelled *Sailing Lake* but too shallow for anything other than row boats, a bending swirl of 326 top-end high-price houses and apartment blocks, water-edge walkways, a mess of bog and tree marked as *wildlife area* – to be overrun by can sucking youths and kids on motorbikes. This is just what Cardiff needs. Take away an irreplaceable facility and give us exclusive residences, space for cars, hundreds of them, lots of private land where the public are not allowed to go, and an end to peace and freedom. The river corridor blocked. The Green Wedge ended. Given up.

Locals are incensed. WPD have ludicrously renamed themselves as Llanishen Water in an attempt to sound user-friendly. A battle fawr rages. The RAG has more posters on poles in gardens, in windows and in the backs of cars than all parties combined during the last general election. Public meetings get filled to capacity. Erudite speakers castigate the planners, the developers, the council which does not listen to its voters, and those ever-present eternal demons, the property developers themselves. They are not wanted but they are here and they stay. If they get defeated then, like those birthday candles you cannot blow out, they burn right back. WPD's first and rejected plan is now in its second incarnation. Twenty houses fewer, some restructuring of road access, and a bit of disingenuousness about protecting waxcaps fungi and rich grassland. If that fails they'll produce another. The protest meetings fill 500 seater lecture theatres and overflow by TV monitor to crowds outside. Politicians rant. People get upset. But developers are deaf. They have their shareholders to consider. Don't they. Their fed faces. Their soft fat hands. Their red necks. Their great space-filled homelands across the sea.

On from here the Green Wedge ploughs north, following the Lleici's course, into the Caerphilly hills. Under City plans the farmland beyond Lisvane, right out to the M4, is due to fill with new housing. The stream will remain, green banks, a spear of breath. But the reservoirs will be lost. In the way of these things development plans, like viruses, keep mutating until they find a weakness which they can exploit. Political will could stop them, but there isn't any. Another Victorian resource demolished. Another opportunity lost. Cardiff's good at that.

CANAL NORTH

The Glamorgan Canal begins in a field just north of Asda at Tongwynlais. There's a pipe which takes water to it from the Taffs Well ridge opposite the Garth. It's a pond of undistinguished rainwater already filled with urban trash. Bike, plastic, bust television, overgrown with ivy duckweed, water starwort, stonewort, blanketweed, spirogyra. The tow-path is tarmac. Someone has spray painted onto it TON SKINS. There are cans in the thickets of Japanese Knotweed. In the high sky the cloud evens up the light. This is the start of what's left of the waterway, of course. A raggy mile of nature reserve[13] set at the outer fringe of the city amid the business parks and the motels and the super-stores.

The Glamorgan and Aberdare Canal was one of the first great inventions of the south Wales industrial age. It ran twenty five and a half miles from the iron works at Merthyr to the sea at Cardiff. It brought down pig iron, then coal. It took ore and timber back. It had fifty one locks and rose 543 feet from sea level. It went up along the Taff valley side to a canal head at Cyfarthfa. The Iron Masters Richard Crawshay and Francis Homfray put up the finance and opened it in 1794. For sixty years, until the decline of iron meshed with the coming of the railways, this canal was the major industrial thoroughfare in Wales. The Marquess of Bute bought it in 1885. His estate managers ran it as a slowly declining concern until deep mining at Merthyr closed the northern section in 1898.

 The canal simply sank as digging below took its foundations away. The same thing happened at Aberdare in 1900 and at Abercynon in 1915. By the end of the Great War traffic was confined to the route between Pontypridd and the Cardiff Sea Lock pound. Small stuff. Independent boatman carrying commercial supplies. Some loose coal to Llandaff Yard and the Patent Fuel works at Maindy. Animal feed. Lime. In 1942 there was a breach in the canal side at Nantgarw. Uneconomic to fix; the death blow. The greater waterway was abandoned. The Sea Lock pound, the mile long canal dock at Cardiff Bay, hung on. It was used by small ships until the 1950s when the dredger Catherine Ethel accidentally pulled the front gate off. The water drained into the Severn Estuary, never to return.[14]

The idea is to walk the route of the Canal from north Cardiff to the sea, follow the line of the old tow path, see what remains. I'm doing it in the company of photographer John Briggs. It's the stuff of anoraks, like collecting railway carriage numbers or writing down the names of pubs without ever going in. Our first problem is deciding where Cardiff actually begins. Politically the border is just north of Tongwynlais. Culturally it's the top of Gabalfa where the Kairdiff accent peters into measured Whitchurch. Or failing that it's Merthyr from where the lads still come on a Friday night for curry and beer. At a dinner I once asked Council Leader and Lord Mayor Russell Goodway where he thought the city ended. Without a blink he told me. Swansea. Greater Cardiff encompasses the entire of south east Wales.

We start at Ironbridge Road, almost the northern border. Behind us is the gap the Taff squeezes through at Taffs Well, Castell Coch guarding the hillside, three iron age burial mounds on the top of Garth Mountain marking the spot on the geomantic grid. There's no interpretation board, just a foot or so of water sitting on the top of a dense silt.

The canal John knows best, the Monmouthshire and Brecon,

which ran to Newport is still full of water, navigable, replete with operating locks and working long boats. You can buy a week on one at Govilon and drift slowly from pub to canal side pub, watching the sky turn from grey to white to grey. In Cardiff the canal has vanished rather like the Mumbles Railway did. Closed, abandoned, then built on. No artefacts kept. No longboat to look at in the Museum. No bridges. The weighlock, the one great relic of industrial south Wales, transported to the Stoke Bruerne Canal Museum in Northamptonshire. A capstan still in the ground halfway down the Nature Reserve and another two in Canal Park where the Sea Lock once was in Cardiff Bay. The waterway has been gone for a mere fifty years and it might as well have never existed.

The section of the Glamorgan which does remain, the one we are on, runs from the M4 / A470 interchange to the site of the old Melingriffith Tin Plate works near Velindre Hospital in Whitchurch. This is the Glamorgan Canal Nature Reserve. Solidly middle class now the sons of toil and their floating boats have gone. Today the path is full of dogs and owners, sticks, children with muddy trainers, someone with a silver scooter, no one with drink or headphones. The canal here used to fill with coal dust delivered by the Taff carrying it from the washeries further north. But now it's clear. Mallard, Moorhen, Kingfisher darting blue, a Sparrow Hawk turning its huge brown wings unexpectedly between the trees. Half way down Forest Lock has been cosmetically restored. Lockgate cemented shut, timber replaced[15], water flowing. Authentic, if you look at it with half-closed eyes. Above us is Longwood Scarp and Whitchurch Hospital then new housing at Holybush.

To the immediate south is the development at Forest Farm Road. Through the trees you can hear the scream of power saws fixing domestic fencing and the rap of hammers installing new kitchens. This is Saturday. The trees are dense and green. Inside the Reserve you can't see a thing.

At the southern end of the Reserve the canal turns under a

re-sited cast iron bridge and vanishes. Culverted back to the river. We
are now on the Taff Trail and the ground is thick with cyclists in day-
glo lycra and double-shelled vented helmets looking like sub-tropical
stick insects. In the verge, half overgrown with ryegrass and thistle, is
an abandoned cast iron canal bridge. Its rounded top rails are cut
deeply with the wear of tow ropes passing over them. Scoring.
Industrial self-harm. We could take it, I tell John. It's been put out with
the rubbish. No one wants it. Let's bring the station wagon round and
try. We don't.

At Llandaff Yard (the Llandaff North of today) remains of industry are scattered along to the eastern edge of Hailey Park. This was
once a great hive with foundry, forge, coal yards, storage, timber
dumps, patent fuel works. Gone with the water. Llandaff North
RFC's Porkies 7s are being played. Big stuff. Banners. Stalls selling
burgers and hot dogs. Chubby players in full kit standing on the
sidelines bearing pints and eating crisps. As a scrum forms a winger
rushes for the corner where someone hands him a lighted Bensons.
He takes a pull and then rushes back.

Meic Stevens, folksinger, lived near here in the 70s when he was
making his break for international stardom with *Outlander,* his great
English-language slice of psychedelia for Columbia. He accosted me
once in Evansfield Road to proclaim that he was now an Anglo-Welsh
writer and a better poet than I would ever be. Could I read some? You
wait, boy, they'll be everywhere soon. But they weren't. And
Outlander sank. Instead his caneuon cymraeg became an enduring
feature of Welsh pop music for four decades. Sain[16] released a tribute
album. Stevens re-recorded his greatest hits and became even more
gnarled to look at. Everyone loves him. And you couldn't imagine
Wales without him. No poems yet in the Anglo-Welsh canon, but
that's a small matter.

South of Llandaff Yard is the Cow and Snuffers which the canal
bent around to run south through Gabalfa. The pub was famously
visited by Disraeli on one of his courting expeditions. It was built in
1812 by landowner Sir Robert Lynche-Blosse and its name is either
a corruption of the Irish *An cu Ar Sndmh* (which means 'The
swimming dog') or the result of a drink-aided competition to find the
most outlandish of names possible for a public house. The Slug and
Lettuce is nothing new.

Walking the Gabalfa estate in boots, shorts, rucksack and camera is a bit like Tom Wolfe found it when accidentally touring Harlem[17]. Opposite of invisible. John is talking about photography. Henri Cartier-Bresson is reputed to have taken 500,000 negatives. That's a 36 shot film every day for fifty years. Never cropped anything. Never used anything but the full frame of his prints. Painter with a palette of light. Black and white recorder of famous and anonymous lives. John pronounces the photographer's name with a convincing Gallic roll. I point my Fuji digital at the Lydstep flats and take a snap into the sun. John doesn't bother. Knows the photograph will be ruined by the light. Doesn't think the weather stained high rises are photogenic. Or both. A youth on a bike too small for him asks what we're doing. Tracking the Glamorgan Canal. What's that?

Gabalfa Cottages would have been near here. Dog sleeping in the short grass. Rebuilt Fiesta driven by a baseball hat. Two girls arguing about how much money is left on their mobile phones. Someone goes past propelling a builder's supply trolley loaded with a stack of shuddering 8x9 lap fence panels. There's no superstore in sight in any direction for at least half a mile. He pushes on along Colwill Road towards the river. We walk south down the long straight towards Mynachdy Lock and the Cambrian Yard Fuel Works. Where they would have been. The Estate landscape, washed by pale white light, is devoid of even the faintest trace of its industrial past.

South of Gabalfa, across the speed-camera blighted Western Avenue and the mall complex that is twenty-four hour Tesco Extra, the trees begin again. The line of the tow path reappears in Sycamore scrub. This is now the Gabalfa Cycleway. Celandines, garlic, bluebell, dog's mercury, knotweed. Puddled woodland floor.

Blackweir, the southernmost of the three weirs on the Taff in Cardiff, lies just to the east of us. Before the barrage the river was tidal as far as here. Bute's West Dock Feeder Canal takes its river water at this spot. Grill, sluice, pile of flotsam, gash wood, plastic. From the Cycleway, canal retaining walls still extant on both sides, we look down to it through the trees. I debate imitating Cartier-Bresson by taking a shower of pictures but in the end leave the camera in the case. Ahead is the long car park that covers the canal's route south to the Castle – my car where we've left it, not vandalised, sandwiches in the boot, and the drive back to where we started.

notes

1. Polluted Pool at Maindee by Jack Crabtree is reproduced on the jacket of *Useful*, Peter Finch's 1997 poetry collection from Seren
2. The site of Longcross Barracks on Newport Road is currently occupied by the CRI, Cardiff's Royal Infirmary. Listed building. Still in partial Health Service use. Most of it abandoned to planning blight. Sign the petition. Re-open our local hospital. Won't happen in my lifetime.
3. The brook is culverted here now, running to the Taff under Lydstep Park.
4. Mynachdy – house of the monk, monastery. These were Manorial lands belonging to Llantarnam but the settlement referred to in the name is lost.
5. Three blocks, 126 flats, lock-up garages not yet bust and rusted, good view of the football pitch and the Draconians changing rooms. A bit weather stained but resistant to urban violence.
6. Now known as Tokyo
7. dsh 1925-1992
8. Collected in Peter Finch, *The End of the Vision*, JJC Ltd, 1970
9. Makoto Ueda, *The Master Haiku Poet Matsuo Bashō* , Twayne Publishers, 1970. For a good introduction to the man, his life and times try the Penguin edition of Basho's *The Narrow Road To The Deep North & other Travel Sketches*.
10. Other than those preserved at St Fagans
11. Cessair – Kesara – was an early Irish earth goddess. A thing to ponder as you drink your Guinness in the Caesar's Arms.
12. WPD (*Llanishen Water* and *Hyder Industrial Group* are subsidiaries) is owned by *Pennsylvania Power and Light Corporation* of Allentown, Pennsylvania.
13. The Glamorgan Canal Nature Reserve with dredged, repaired canal opened in 1967
14. The Sea Lock pound, the canal basin, became a rubbish dump until it was filled in 1959 and developed into the Hamadryad play area and park.
15. In 1988, using recycled green-heart timber from Sheffield, and local cement.
16. Sain, the Welsh language record label – www.sain.wales.com
17. Tom Wolfe, *Bonfire of the Vanities*, Farrar, Straus and Giroux, 1987

SOUTH

CANAL SOUTH

I meet John Briggs in the sun at the ambulance station end of the
North Road car park, right next to the pay and display machine
(unvandalised) on a surface drifted with horse chestnut detritus,
cigarette packets and road dust. We are continuing south along the
route of the Glamorgan Canal vanished into the cityscape almost
without trace. This is the place in the waterway's long descent to the
sea where the tow path changed sides to protect the privacy of Bute
and his lands. The railings that protect the car park's western side are
early Victorian, oxidized, set in blocks of Radyr stone. Where the
canal ran is now tarmac car park and red surfaced cycleway. Both are
swamped by a sonic wash of diesel and revving saloon from North
Road itself. As ever there's no indicator of what this space once was.
The Portacabin used by the attendant is like a prefab lock keeper's
hut. I could have caught fish from my little window, he says when I
tell him just where his hut is located. But there would have been no
canal fish, of course, too much black dust. While the industrial
revolution steamed nothing lived in those waters.

Near the Castle by the Bute Park gates, a thatched keepers house
stood until it was bombed flat by the Germans. Beside it was the
North Road stone wharf. Here Pennant sandstone from Pontypridd
was offloaded before being dressed on site and incorporated as paving
and kerb into Cardiff's streets. No traces discernable now. Cleared.
Filled in, resurfaced, restructured, the whole place made new, flame-
throwered clean of its past. This spot is Cardiff's psychic centre. The

place around which the city
revolves. South of government,
north of commerce, west of
residence, east of sport and river
and space. It's the centre by not
being any of these things.
Nowhere near the docklands, the
hills, the offices of our administration, what's left of our
industry, but equidistant from
them all. Stand here and be
Cardiff. I'm about to explain this
to John but he's found the city's

last remaining fragment of actual canal evidence – the North Road underpass. He photographs the stone work and the lines, similar to those seen on the abandoned bridges further north, cut into the ironwork by a century of tow ropes. This is Thomas Dadford's[1] 1794 canal arch under Kingsway. They've built toilets at one end next to a giant ventilation inlet fan for

the Cardiff Hilton. John moves a Macdonalds wrapper to improve his shot. After he's pressed the shutter he carefully puts the litter back.

At the farrside of the underpass we climb back up to emerge at the top of the Friary, a bustle of cafés, aluminium street seats, a sandwich board advertising Bar Cuba's Bacardi B-Bar with Salsa Lessons 8-10 every Tuesday. Two skateboarders. Bronze-faced administrators striding, their briefcases and their handhelds. Valley kids in all-white track suits, tattooed midriffs, nose rings. Pensioners on the City's temporary street benches. No hard goods you can buy. Just consumables. Portacoffee, Danish, fast food, Italian biscuits. Buskers. Temporary fencing, stacked paving brick, diggers. Queen Street gets resurfaced. A net of history as Town Wall, East Gate, Town Pump, bear pit and slaughterhouse meet. The canal was tunnelled under to emerge south in what's now the Queen's Arcade. It ran the length of the town's east ditch, rounding Cock's Tower[2] to plough on through the centre of MVC and emerge at Cardiff's Amsterdam – the confluence of Bridge Street, Caroline Street and The Hayes.

On the way John snaps not so much the route but its inhabitants. His photographs are always full of people. Demure female security guards. Big Issue sellers. Shoppers. In the Hayes' café quarter John is completely at home. His photographs of the old open air market which operated here thirty years ago are famous[3]. J. O'Connell Vegetable Specialist. The Snackbar Café. The New Moon. The Costa Rica Coffee Company. The pervading odour from Brain's Caroline Street Brewery. Workers, watchers. The Jack London hustle of smell and sweat. Today the surfaces have been scraped clean, rejigged, grassed, fenced, lit, re-coloured. Gone, all of it. We target the Custom House and walk on.

The Custom House, appropriately on Custom House Street (or Heol-y-Tollty yn gymraeg) has sculptor Brain Fell's giant clenched fists outside it. The building has been preserved and is currently half vacant. The Dragon's Rugby Trust occupy a corner. The deserted York Hotel abuts at the back. The Terminus, the pub, once faced the statue of Bute on his plinth, the monument[4]. Trolley buses terminated here. You asked the conductor for The Monument. He knew where you meant. St Mary Street reached the London rail link. Here was Dadford's magnificent Romanesque iron bridge which bore the arms of both Lord Bute and the City of Cardiff. It marked the top of the widened canal. The waterway at this spot took on a whole new shape and purpose. Below East and West Canal Wharfs the canal widened to become a dock. Ship water bending south to the sea lock and the tidal Channel. Why it is so far north.

We find a track through the development of Callaghan Square to take us along Canal Parade and on into Canal Park. The waterway is recalled, for once, in extant street names. John looks for evidence of the timber floats, the junction canal to Bute's West Dock, the ship dry docks, the iron ore wharfs, the steam packet station, sail lofts, brickyards, ship builders. But they are all gone. This was originally swamp land. Stone ballast unloaded from arriving ships once formed a quarter of a mile long ridge. It was used for building or thrown into the sinking mud as hard core. Purpose in everything. A century and a half of arriving rock used as the foundation for blossoming

ButeTown.

Canal Park is completely deserted. No wreckage evident. Vandalism fixed. At least faster now than it once was. To our left ButeTown being rebuilt piecemeal. Along the black corrugated fence of the western side are the still highly discernable slogans from the Lynette White campaigns. THE BOYS ARE INNOCENT. FREE THE CARDIFF THREE. According to local historian Neil Sinclair this area is the real Tiger Bay, the residences surrounding Loudoun Square. North is town. The houses to the south are the residential Docks. What's left of them. The community is multi-racial, tight knit, suspicious of incomers, Arab hat, black veiled, fast car. You still get occasional shootings. You get them everywhere.

South of James Street there's a community mural erected on the supposed site of the sea lock, the place where the canal entered the sea. The maps I have show that the lock was further south. John reminisces about a pub called the New Sea Lock which once stood at the end of nearby Harrowby Street, next to the sand wharfs. He had his stag night there in 1981. The pub lasted until excavations for the new groundwater pumping station undermined the foundations and the place had to be pulled down. Nearest now is the bar of the five star St David's Hotel. You can get in with no tie but try it in working trousers. Beer is £2.85 a half. No one I know has ever been brave enough to order a pint.

The actual sea lock, the place where the canal formally ended, was at the top of what remains of Penarth Terrace, west end of Windsor Esplanade. The coast here has moved south by at least fifty meters. Alluvium. A new sea wall now holds back a barrage trapped freshwater Bay. There's an interpretation board and boardwalk wetlands being developed south of that. We open the map and try to pin-point what used to be, and where. This wall is chamfered. That's not. Clear proof. By Jove, Holmes, says John, I do believe you are right.

Across the flat bay, stacked with boats, litter scooped out, aerated, weedless, is the line of the barrage. Lock machinery. Pumps. Observation towers. Windbreaks in the form of ship's sails. The brightly coloured land train, ex-Ebbw Vale Garden Festival now Cardiff Bay tourist attraction, toots along its top. John took a group of aged Cardiff seafarers on this as an outing last week. You get 'Land of My Fathers', massed choirs and Bryn Terfel plus Keith from

Splott (the driver) giving you the glossy history through the carriage speakers, says John. Lots of commentary on the way out. Nothing on the way back.

A yacht slides past us, so slowly. Industry replaced by endless leisure.

ELY FIELDS

Where the Ely meets the Taff has always been indeterminate. River mouths move as if they were speaking. Silt accumulates then shifts. The rivers themselves meander. In Cardiff's heyday the Ely looped here like a Hindu snake. Railtracks crossed the peninsula to the Victoria Wharf coal-stays on the tidal harbour. Penarth Dock station watched from the far side. Grime and sweat. The substance big cities are made from. By the 1960s the industry had gone and the wooden wharfs had begun to crumble. The Ely meanders were abandoned in 1971 and the river diverted through a new straight channel cut along their western edge. The river now ran parallel to the Cogan railway. Revealed hollows were used as landfill. The ancient Penarth Moors became a dump for city garbage. By the 1990s the hollows were full, capped with three-feet of impervious clay and redeveloped as Grangemoor Parc with the Cardiff Bay Retail Park alongside. South East lay the Ferry Road peninsula, the Red House, the Cardiff Bay Yacht Club, and the site for the in-coming Sports Village and attendant housing. To the south west, up Dunleavy Drive, are Ely Fields.

Ely Fields? Secret, gated Cardiff. A thirty-acre triangle of land with the river front on its long side and the elevated Grangetown Link and Cogan Spur roadways on the others. Peer into it as you drive past, most you'll see are trees.

This is home to the exclusive Grangemoor Court waterfront apartments (£160,000 plus for a one bedroomed flat at 2004 prices) and Cardiff's much-vaunted Celtic Gateway Media Park. WDA, Rhodri, suits and smiles. Who creates these names? No park, no gateway, and hardly Celtic. Penarth mud, drained. But the media are here. NTL's bespoke 65,000 square foot call-centre with its glazed atria and softly curving maritime roof gleams white on the green sward[5]. Opposite is BT's prize ninety-million-pound Internet Data 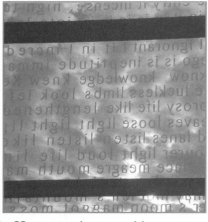 Centre (IDC). Known as Elinia House, and now sold on to an investment bank, the complex is run by BT Global Services. No sign anywhere of the rolling silt mud that this place once was. South is water. Sky is blue. In the sun it feels like the Mediterranean.

The glass front of the IDC is riddled with words[6]. High over the revolving entrance run a series of names: *Peter Pan Tinkerbell Roger Ellis Norman Schwenk D.Z. Phillips William Carlos Williams William ap Will William Williams Jones Walcott St Paul ap Iestyn A.M. Allchin.* Norman, poet, hat wearer, and American denizen of the Cardiff literary scene for at least forty years hasn't seen his name up here yet. Nether has Roger Ellis, nor, come to that, has Peter Pan, William Carlos Williams nor A.M. Allchin. These are all fragments of my long web poem, *R.S. Thomas Information*, never published in hard copy form but now here, hard as you like and in copious quantity, all over BT's Bay masterpiece. I've parked my car on the roadside under the Link Road bridge. The official car parks are all chain fenced and motor barriered. The service roads look vulnerable, park and someone will remove your vehicle with a rocket launcher. Or tow it away for scrap. At the entrance a uniformed guard tells me that I can't just turn up here, I need an appointment. These buildings are not like offices. They are not[7]. Inside the lobby is all curves and glass and R.S. Thomas deconstructed. *Risk ripening rescued red random rubbing reborn R. rooting rnld ring remote rain rain rooting roof reason remoter root removes roses return rigid.* Three hundred people a day will walk past it. *fescue fuddled females flame fire flies flying failed flowed from fields foolish fields foolish.* This is data in action. You look at it. You read it. You don't take it in.

Back in the early 80s when the best home computer in the world was the BBC B with 32k memory, no printer and a cassette-tape A-drive I wrote a program in Basic which would compose Anglo-Welsh poems for me. I set up a number of word pools containing the sort of vocabulary the Anglo-Welsh were famous for – sheep, stipple, cariad, hillside, hiraeth, chapel, pit – and then a couple of rules for how these words could be combined. Up it all came on screen.

slate fences on farmer's hillsides,
shrouded cockles and grass-polished deacons,
the nation majestically watered

This was great. Machines that could do your work for you. I copied the poetry down.

R.S. Thomas, Wales' greatest poet, dour and dark, was clearly next. He was a Cardiffian who had deserted the anglicised-city for the north. He'd learned Welsh to perfection and adopted a hard, revolutionary line on the culture. A man who certainly needed to be celebrated. I chose the most contemporary of devices open to me. The net. Using real and imagined sources I build up a hyperlinked database of the poet's history, his friends and acquaintances, his fans, his influences, his childhood, his favoured lexicon. We are all identifiable by the extent of our vocabulary and the frequency of its use. What would his look like? I found out. In his lifetime he was nominated for the Nobel Prize. He didn't get it. I wrote the history up. Did he ever listen to Mozart? Certainly. Dion and the Belmonts? Maybe not. He was a famous birder but not of the reworked feather-bearers I included. *Greeebe Hebron Goshandy Goosehandy Gobbler Grey Dipper Kingklank Goldeneye Grodfish Godeel Golders Green Grass Basher h'm.*

The database – the poem – grew like topsy. I built in a bibliographic resource showing his extant books and where to buy them. There was a newspaper story somewhere about him looking happy. I inserted a clickable link. I wrote an imaginary walk of his through fields of mangles and an encounter with the poet Childe Roland[8] Someone e-mailed me to say that R.S. had moved to Criccieth. I pasted it in. The piece was structured alphabetically to give it a base.

I mixed genuine R.S. vocabulary with imagined resources and developed a host of cross-cutting links. When you arrived at the site there was no intention that you should read the data sequentially, A to Z. Far from it. This was a simulacrum of the real world where data was to be grazed and processed, batched and filed, cut and pasted, spliced and dumped. Visitors took it as how life was. His son Gwydion said the work was elliptical. R.S. himself would have been appalled.

Back out in the Bay the heat is burning the shirt into my back. Along the edges of the undeveloped areas of the site ragwort, wild carrot and yellow toadflax sprout. Inside the IDC data hovers. R.S. on the windows, R.S. in the cable, R.S. on the central servers. Data developed and deployed. R.S. of the new age. Wouldn't have been appreciated. I know.

BARRAGE

It's eight miles to go right around water-filled Cardiff Bay. Conjoined river mouths and estuary frontage. For Bute's decades and those of the declining Port that followed him this was all shining mud, most of the time. Cardiff's tidal fall at 14 metres is highest anywhere outside the Bay of Fundy[9]. Ships had to rush past the banks of Cefn y Wrach (the witches back) when the waters flowed. Get into dock while they had the chance. The Barrage, at more than a kilometre long, holds back 500 acres of water. The output of the two rivers – fresh water. Full of pollutants opponents claimed: run-offs, sewage, and mess. Algal blooms. Small flies. Tiny things. During the years of the project's proposal and then its construction it has been dogged by controversy. The Bay was originally a designated SSSI (Site of Special Scientific Interest). The wading birds feeding off mud-dwelling invertebrates were unique to

the region. Redshanks. Dunlins. Plover. Moving them would be hard. They were offered new wetlands up the coast. Developers had a hard time evicting them. Telling them just where they had to go. You'd think an SSSI was immovable. Can I have planning permission to put up a new house on the dock side? No. Well how about a billion gallon total immersion followed by total knockdown and rebuild? Certainly, why not.

Fears ran wide and wild. Groundwater would rise and the entire of working class south of Cardiff would have their foundations flooded. Disease would be rampant. The lagoon would go black and stink. Algae would encroach our drinking water. Sand from our pleasure beaches to the west would wash to the Atlantic and be lost. Fish would vanish. The railink would subside as its track became undermined. Grangetown would return to salt marsh. Canton to quagmire. Rats would gather. Plague. Dark deeds. The Bute Tunnel would flood. Tall buildings would sink and topple. Cardiff – the disaster movie. None of this happened.

The Barrage itself is huge. Built with fish passes, locks for boats, water exits, landing stages, control towers, sluice gates, bascule bridges, road, walkway. Half way across the city have built a shelter which resembles the sails of a ship. They sell tea and ice cream here at high summer. The banks are grass planted. Salt-liking shrubs. Children playing among them. Men with brushes sweep the walkway. Joggers run along the top. You can't drive the route yet. There's a car park at the Penarth end. 50p. And a gate where the Barrage reaches Queen Alexandra Dock. Word is that once APB have tidied up the Port a little they'll open it. But that time is not yet.

I'm walking across with Morgan, who, at high speed, is giving me a story about coming through the Barrage on day two after impoundment and crashing into the side of the brand new lock. Couldn't turn the marine engine off. His friend, the owner, had gone out shopping and instead of potatoes had bought a boat. Hadn't told his wife.

Joined the yacht club. Had a time getting the hang of it. When faced with the Bay's enormous sea lock went to bits. Couldn't stop roaring forward. Morgan's stories often have an air of urban fantasy. Did you sink? No. Scraped the Barrage, and the boat. I think there might have been some shouting. Without a doubt.

We're standing above that same lock watching pleasure craft and boatloads of sea fishermen return with the tide. The mud flats are still there but outside the Barrage rather than in. Swarms of gulls and cormorant swoop and dive. Brown water oozes then rushes and turns.

The enterprise has cost £197 million and without it Cardiff Bay's development as up-market apartment housing estate and old person's holiday destination just wouldn't exist. Walking it is full of sea air, views of Penarth and its pier, St David's Hotel with its landed seagull, the hard-hat Wales Millennium Centre, the white and tiny point of the almost totally fake Norwegian Church. But as a construction it no more takes your breath away than a reservoir might. Dam, tower, concrete, water, swirling birds, sheets of foam.

Hamadryad Park

Not finished when I went through the
blue gates. Ship sails pinned to them.
Past the metal railings fashioned from
metal rope. The peninsular where Bute met
Grangetown and the Canal sluiced
to the sea. From the headland
the walled communities of Lower Grange
and Windsor Quay watch each other.

Merc facing thrashed Fiesta. Bin bag wrecked
bus shelter. Pushchair with broken
wheels. Time and space for this seafaring life.
Someone with an air rifle shoots a heron gull. A
can of trash comes out of a fifth floor window.
Under the veneer the mudflats sink

At the exhibition there are shots of Bute Town
as it used to be. B&W dust. Streets with hardly
a car between them. Grey faces downing dark

beer in the Packet and the White Hart. A docklands
community at the end of its life.

In James Street someone has torched a Ford. It is
doused and hustled from existence faster than a
body. Isn't allowed to smear the value of the
rising ash-floored apartments. The White Hart
still does bitter but also white wine in fluted glass.

A docker's ghost rounds the corner, doing the
run between Big Windsor and Casablanca, one work shirt
tail outside his trousers, pint in his hand.

No good. Nostalgia is for the aged. The New Sea Lock
is gone. And the Yardarm. You remember
me, I say to Frankie Johnston, big hat, lounging outside
the betting shop. You do. I used to come down here
in my youth. Everyone knew me. He looks at me slowly.
Up, then down. No, shakes his head, no I don't.

COUNTY HALL

I'm in the sloping front of lobby of County Hall. Curved reception with
visible computers, brown and cream window frames, glass and views
of the water. The future in 1984 when the building opened but already
looking slightly jaded. There's a wall hanging of miners with lamps,
printed circuit boards for the futuristic touch, and what looks like
Caerphilly Castle but with its south east tower not leaning out of true.
Old Land Of My Fathers So Dear Unto Me it says along the bottom.
County Hall. Centre of Cardiff's Government. Hub and dynamo.

As a building the Hall was in the avant garde. It was designed by
County Architect, J.R.C. Bethel, and erected in the centre of the devas-
tated and workless docks at a time when confidence was at its lowest
ebb. The population imagined that Cardiff was twinned with Nizhni
Novgorod, moving ever deeper into decay, depression and darkness.
The Hall's pagoda-like structure, overhanging black-slated roofs, four
sides around a central court, three stories rising to five towards the
water, gives it a subdued dignity. Local power through orange-brown
brick. Nerve not lost when faced with Thatcher's years of closure.

Before 1984, South Glamorgan's several hundred staff had enjoyed a clerical life in the Hodge Building on Newport Road. Easy access, two minutes walk to the town centre and an overkill of shopping. Who'd want to work in the distant Bay among the broken and the deserted? They all shifted, however, and for at least a decade their new home stood in glorious isolation with

only the red-brick Pier Head Building for company. Cars got broken into, a few of them. There were the occasional confrontations between locals and clerks from Caerphilly and Nantgarw in the Ship and Pilot and the Baltimore and the Yardarm. But the move worked. Still works, now, as flagship for Cardiff County Council[10]. Powerbase, house of the people.

The Council's controversial Leader has a penthouse office overlooking the long sweep of East Dock's water. Russell Goodway, man of the people, the working class, the trade unions. Double-breasted blazer, round florid faced like the laughing policeman. Hounded by the local papers and the Welsh Assembly Government for a stream of A-list style, irrelevant misdemeanours – why does he live in Barry and not the City? Why doesn't he let the Lord Mayor have untrammelled access to the Mansion House? Why are his allowances so high? Who cares? With Goodway things get done. If he were a different age and shape they'd probably arrange to photograph him on the beach at St Tropez wasting his travel allowance or complain that he dined at Woods instead of Harry Ramsden's. In the June 2004 Council elections, Goodway's Labour Party lost control of Cardiff Council. Russell held his Ely ward by a mere 62 votes. He now plans to become a vicar in the Church in Wales.

He got into politics by accident, he tells me. Drinking in the Wenvoe Arms one night back in the days when getting someone to bother to actually stand in a local election was more of an issue than the election itself, he was put upon. Do us a favour. You won't get in. The seat has been Tory for too long. A South Glamorgan ward that merged parts of Canton with Llandaff. 1985. The miners finished. Be Tory or die. But by the slimmest of majorities Russell got elected. It was Cardiff by chance. He could have stood for anywhere in South Glam, the Vale, Barry, Penarth. But the City's magnets were already at work. Under local government reorganisation Cardiff became a unitary authority in 1995. Goodway as leader. The city turning its lights back on.

It used to be dark in Cardiff, when I was younger, he tells me. Grey buildings, black skies. No one had any confidence. There was no work. East Moors had just closed. Cardiff was a place where companies had branches, if they were here at all. No one was actually based in the city. I remember being asked once by a young mother if I thought her son would be good enough to work in an office. The limit of her expectation, let alone her aspiration, was her boy taking up a clerical career. I had to change that.

Russell's device was to persuade those people in Cardiff who spend money to spend it in a way that promoted the City's own agenda. Cardiff would become a European Capital City – like Barcelona, Cologne, Düsseldorf and Rotterdam. A place linked to its catchment. A place where people would come for entertainment, for shopping, for fun; a place where deals would be made and wheels would spin. City as regional hotbed. The economy of the hinterland would depend on Cardiff. Cardiff and its Valleys. Cardiff and its coastlands. Cardiff and its Vale. Half the population of Wales live within the travel to work area of Cardiff. That makes the Capital more significant than the region itself. City as state. But a cosmopolitan Capital for Wales rather than of Wales. Many cultured. And we don't make enough of this. Russell wants to do more. And how do we relate to Wales' tribal north West? I don't ask this and Russell doesn't say.

Generally his plans have worked. The Millennium Stadium, a seventy-thousand capacity sports arena sits in the city centre. The Millennium Centre is about to open. Work has begun on the Sports Village. The Barrage is in place. The Assembly is here. Financial institutions and international corporations are moving to the city. 13,000 people employed in the entertainment, food and hotel trade. More than two steelworks. Palpable confidence. The cluster is growing.

There have been mistakes. Boulevard de Nantes should never have been allowed to bisect the Civic Centre at Cathays Park from the City itself. From Queen Street you should have been able to see

City Hall. The Canal should have been kept. East Dock should not have been sealed from the sea. No ships possible now, unless you crane them in. And the Castle's Animal Wall has to be put back where Burges and Bute wanted it, in front.

There are other changes planned, to be taken forward by Russell's successor. St David's Two, the razing of south central Cardiff in the pursuance of shopping, everything from the Hayes to the Prison, will rocket Cardiff back up the UK retail league. Currently the City is Number 8, dropped from 6, now that Birmingham has redeveloped its Bull Ring. New bridge across the Taff south of the railway, Dumballs to Taff Embankment. Wood Street pedestrianised. A convention and exhibition centre wrapped around the southern end of the Stadium. Transport hub straight to conference, expo or big game. Heritage trails developed and mapped. City Museum. Science Park near the Roath Dock Basin. National Theatre. National Art Gallery on the site of the old Tram Shed, back of Tudor Road. Eastern link road running from the Bay to the M4 built. Fast highway to the airport.

But most importantly Russell wants to see a shift of emphasis from physical structure to social structure, from form to content, from how it looks to how it is. Improve services, simplify configuration, attract the great Academies here, involve young people. City region. A future world of urban space cut by green corridors. The City Government, as it now calls itself, has produced a White Paper, *Building For Our Future, The New 2020 Vision*[11], outlining plans. No mention of scandal, error and excessive profit taking. No corruption. No useable past lost in the cause of corporate pocket lining. Can it be done? Russell thinks yes.

But he's a politician, he would.

I'm back heading north, into the older city. Two miles on lies the white portland City Hall, original centre of Capital governance. Thousands of visitors have had themselves taxied there rather than to the Bay's pagoda. Hundreds of others have found themselves shivering in the hard-to-get-to Bay when they were meant to be at a meeting or a wedding reception in leafy Cathays Park. Thirty minutes walk from the recently new to the refurbished old. City all the way.

WALES MILLENNIUM CENTRE

It used to be the Bute East Dock basin, between Maritime Road and Britannia Road, Roath Basin south of it, Dock Offices to the west. Now it's the Millennium Centre, armadillo on a bed of hardcore. The waters drained. The Dock Offices washed red-brick clean and reborn as Pier Head Building. The Assembly's interpretation centre. Focus for Cardiff, clock tower on the BBC evening news like a Welsh Big Ben. To say that this place has been a long time coming is to severely understate it. It's been half a century. Rattled with controversy, resistance, connivance, rivalry and resignation. But it's here now. 2000 seats. Jonathan Adams' storm-defying piece of essentially-Welsh, landmark architecture. Is it like bend-wall Bilbao? High-rise New York? Glass-wave London? No. It's steel and glass and slate and ancient timber and, at the back, walls six-stories high of what looks like creosoted lapwood fencing. It's Wales. Not England. What we have. How we are.

It sits slightly to the left of the Oval Basin, the rather unfittingly named Roald Dahl Plass, its brutal red brick facing down the Assembly's Crickhowell House, focus of Lloyd George Avenue, shouting up James Street, visible from everywhere – Penarth Head, the east Port, UCI Car Park, County Hall debating chamber. A victory. Back in 1897 they were going to build a pier carrying a rail link here[12]. Shoved out into the estuary to service passenger liners. White whales with their rich cargos. The ships never came. The pier never got built.

In the mid-1990s – Barrage yet to open, Bay yet to drown – the prospect of a Roald Dahl Centre for Children's Literature briefly surfaced. In the style of Foster's City Hall for London, the centre was to sit out in the water, swimming the wind at the end of a snaking causeway. A Welsh Statue of Liberty welcoming yachts and sand dredgers and the RMS St Helena as they washed into the roaring Bay of the Tiger. Children would visit. Matilda, Charlie and the BFG would be celebrated. Dahl would live on. But money didn't arrive to support such a landmark project. Instead it's being built inland, and in far less exotic style, at Great Missenden, Buckinghamshire. Due to open in 2005.

Opera has been the driver. WNO[13] narrowly missed having a house built in the National Museum of Wales courtyard. Town centre performances, but cramped. Instead a Millennium Commission-backed competition was launched for a grand Opera House in the Bay. There were over 500 entries. Manfredi Nicoletti, Norman Foster and Itsuko Hasegawa became popular choices but Iraqi Zaha Hadid won. We were to have a world class structure, angles and spikes, from an acclaimed avant garde architect. The elite were entranced. The people hated it. Local red-tops drummed up a storm of protest. Cost rose. The Millennium Commission queried the business plan. It was discovered that Hadid had previously only ever actually built a fire station. Sir Geoffrey Inkin, chairman of CBDC[14] travelled to Weil am Rhein in Germany to see it and came back with a face of thunder. Someone even suggested that Hadid wasn't formally registered as an architect. Things went from dark to black. The plan sank. Tearing of hair. Dismay and disgust. Nicholas Crickhowell, Secretary of State for Wales with a reputation on the line and a huge Hadid supporter, wrote the full story as a book. *Opera House Lottery*[15]. University of Wales Press, 1997. A rollicking read but remaindered three years later.

The need for a Bay centrepiece wouldn't go away. Planners cast around for a substitute. In 1996 a scheme for an Opera House successor, the Wales Millennium Centre, was launched. Fronted by Sir Alan Cox, former Chairman of Allied Steel and Wire and an arts supporter of some note, considerable courage and a negotiating style that got through bomb-proof doors, the plans were adventurous. They proposed a 2000-seat lyric theatre, an Imax cinema, a Museum of the Sea, and a south Wales home for the Welsh league of youth, the Urdd (complete with on-site youth hostel). A bunch of assorted arts

orgs would also be shoehorned in. A greater Opera House with voter-friendly added value. All boxes ticked. "This Centre is going to hold its arms out to the people and say 'come on in'" ran the promotional brochure. Percy Thomas were the architects. Their first-shot sketch looked like a branch of British Home Stores with a high rise glass sail on the south western corner. Uncontroversial. In the extreme. Who could say no?

By the time the plan had congealed, in the way of multi-million pound proposals, into something that might actually be built, the Museum and the Imax had gone. They'd been replaced by Diversions Dance. The arts orgs were literature agency, the Academi; Hi-Jinx Theatre; and WAMF, the Welsh Amateur Music Federation. This group were joined later by the Touch Trust, an art therapy charity. Through the fog ethnic providers and celtic centres drifted and bumped but never solidified. The plan was set. In co-operation with partner Percy Thomas, Welshman Jonathan Adams was appointed as architect. They couldn't have picked a better man.

Jonathan's plan was to make the building reflect the land it came from, the country it stood for, the place it was in. The roof – the great curving helmet – would be steel, after Cardiff's long life as a producer. The sides would be faced with slate waste shipped down from Blaenau Ffestiniog. The walls would rise in staggered layers like the rock strata at Nash Point. Glass would be from Swansea. There would be a great poem across the entrance, written in windows, done in Romano-British lettering, in the style of David Jones[16]. Light would pour from them up James Street. The roof would have gardens and terraces planted with wind-bent tress like those along Glamorgan's Heritage coast. Inside, steel columns would rise imprinted with tree fern fossils from the depths of the coalfield. Light, sound and landscape memory. All the references were right. The plan – with a couple of management hiccups, the jettisoning of the roof garden, and a general floor-area shrinkage in order to fit available budgets – went ahead. Building started in 2000. The centre opened in 2004.

From the roof top, mid 2003, hard hat and notebook, I can see the whole of the Bay like a map. I've reached here up an unfinished stair-well followed by a wooden ladder. You can only go up if you've a real head for heights, I'm told. I have, I lie. The steel roof panels are being installed by contractors who abseil down the dome's precipitous slant on nylon rope. When the wind gets higher than a light breeze they have to stop. The steel would airplane. Fly off through Bute Town History and Arts rear windows. Slice the lamp heads from the Oval basin's light columns. Hover with the gulls.

The foundation stone, in a colonnade on the ground floor, way below me, has travelled too. Connected the north with the south. Made Wales whole. Its journey, an extended PR stunt, involved lugging a slab of Welsh slate from its origins in Penrhyn Quarry,

Bethesda all the way to Cardiff Bay using as near to nineteenth century transport methods as possible[17]. To add spice, Grahame Davies was commissioned to accompany it and poetically write the journey up.

The slate has been squared and smoothed and tastefully and bilingually engraved[18] by Ieuan Rees. It's in a padded wooden crate, shrouded like a weapon of mass destruction, waiting for the horse and trap to cart it to the narrow-gauge rail head at Blaenau Ffestiniog. From here it will roll by gravity and by steam down to the quayside at Porthmadog, a step from Cob Records, largest second-hand CD shop in the world. At the dock it will transfer to the veteran schooner Vilma and sail, as slate always used to, out into the Irish Sea, south around the squalls of Pembrokeshire's Cape Horn and then up the foggy Bristol Channel, navigating sandbanks and rip tides, to gloriously enter Cardiff Bay at high water, in full sun with trumpets sounding. Great plan. But this is January. Out there to south west, where the seas fall off the end of the world, the storms are furiously anti-cycling.

Grahame is waiting. He's stuck, snug, in the cabin of the Vilma. Confined to Porthmadog port for the night. On his own and no sailor. He fancies some chips, can see the lights of High Street. Decides to disembark, leans over the side to pull up the row boat, like he's been told to, his link with the shore. Vodafone from his top pocket slides out and vanishes into the inky water. Undaunted Grahame scrambles into the boat, slops and slides, rows warily for the quay. Can't find a place to tie up. Slithers in the dark. Grabs a ring, loops the rope. Up, swaying, out, lights, smells, greasy chrome, chips, comfort, then back through the wet swaying darkness to the waiting Vilma and his lonely copy of *Historic Shipwrecks of Wales*. Does Grahame know something we don't? Beyond the harbour the winds blow. Does he relish the storm and roaring white water out there? No. Definitely not.

Colours available – Heather Blue, Heather Red, Heather Grey, Blue Grey, Dark Blue Grey, Vermont Green, Autumn Green, Mottled

Purple, Truthville Red. Last four not used. Impermeable. Non-combustible. Unaffected by UV light. Unaffected by vegetable growth, rot or insect attack. Unaffected by freezing. Unaffected by atmospheric pollution, sea air and sea spray[19].

Plan B is to fly the thing south by helicopter. Grahame, goggles, headphones, joins the flight on the sands at Morfa Bychan and it's over almost as soon as it has started. Wales like a TV programme. Cardiff's heliport on Foreshore Road looming into sight. Camera. News inserts. Grahame smiling with the packing case. His 26th interview in three days. It's all gone wrong, hasn't it? Not at all. Grahame is smilingly upbeat in his response. To ensure that the illusion is maintained he slides home for the night and returns the following morning to join Bryn Terfel and a crew of reporters and cameramen on a RNLI inflatable at the entry to the Barrage. There's the slate, boxed, in the inflatable's interior. They sail through the lock and approach the Inner Harbour. Massed gentry. Media. Dignitaries. Flags. School choirs. Pianists. The First Minister. The Chairman. The Board. Russell Goodway. Jonathan Adams. Jan Morris covering it for the *New Statesman*. The choir sings. Bryn Terfel praises them. Grahame smiles and waves. The stone is off-loaded and transferred by fork lift to its final resting place on the Centre's northern corner. Focus of Lloyd George Avenue, the true start of the Taff Trail. The sun shines. Everyone cheers.

Plan C was to have an exact duplicate driven south in the boot of a fast car. At sea the original could have gone overboard and sunk. Could have taken too long to sail south. Might have been diverted to Milford Haven to avoid incoming storms. Could have been dropped and smashed and chipped and broken. Maybe the finished stone stood in its replica packaging in an on-site pre-fab the whole time while the musical drama was performed beyond it. Everyone I've asked denies it. And if I knew I'd deny it too.

I'm standing near the Academi's offices on Pier Head Street with the WMC's hard red, tight and taut brickwork behind me. To my right are the fences surrounding the construction cranes putting up the Assembly's new Debating Chamber. To my left the swirl of mud and Portacabin that will soon be the building site for the Arts Pod, WMC's final component. The wind is cold. A raggle of parents with placards and gaily dressed children picket the Assembly's revolving doored entrance. Rain arrives in squalls. Nearly finished. Yes. And when it's done it'll be glorious.

THE BUTE EAST AND ATLANTIC WHARF

The Bute East Dock is called Atlantic Wharf[20] on the Agents' plans. They're selling apartments at a new property they're calling *City Wharf*, top of the dock, eastern corner, on a footprint about the size of a corner shop. Onto this they've managed to cantilever eight stories. The name is vital. No *Caerdydd* anything. No mention of Dock either. Far too redolent of work and smoke and coal and pain. Wharf has an air of sophistication about it. Money, glass, water, leisure. The essential elements. We are not selling to the middle-class family market here. Mallards Reach won't do. These blonde-floored, curved-walled habitats will sell to urban singles, opinion formers, city investors, no kids, no pets. Designer shoes. Fast cars. £2000 annual service charge (rising) to guard the gate and sweep the common passage ways. Proximity to water is auspicious.

The Dock, Bute's second in Cardiff's great period of industrial expansion, opened without ceremony in 1859. 45 acres, 30 coal staiths, 25 hydraulic cranes, 3 graving docks, 9370 feet of quayage. Lots of water. The Fear Not. The Lady Havelock. North Star. The Lilian. The Helen Burns. Zimi. Tweed. Cardiff Castle. Telemarco. Hipparchus. Ocean Pearl. Alaska. Star of Gwent. Flying Scud. Star of the Taff. Hellespont. Little Annie. Kings Oak. Red Rose. Earl of Dunraven. Mardy. Mecca. Medina. Alarm. Vectic. Velindra. Wenvoe. Roath. Cardiffian. The first ship in was The Mananiello, low in the water, carrying coal. The dock was connected to Bute's earlier West Dock by a junction canal and to the open water by sea gates. The

National Assembly's office suite and the south end of the Wales Millennium Centre now fill that space. Sea trade is over. For Cardiff anyway[21].

Just to the east of City Wharf, other side of the Central Link road fly-over, is a small industrial wasteland accessed by a slip road running from the Tyndall Street roundabout. This land was Rhymney railyard until the sixties clearances. Wagon

builders[22]. Saw mill. Creosote works. Tramway. Timber yard. Tar and resin distillery. Today – I'm visiting in early 2003 – it holds just about all that's left of what hands-dirty work there is in the city – Pogson & Sons Crankshaft Grinders, Machinery Movements Cranes. All of them with notice to quit. Shifted east to new sites on the Wentloog flatlands, city fringes, marshland chasing them. I need to put half a ton of hard core into this yard each year, Derek the crane yard owner tells me. The ground sinks beneath us. They've done the ten meter bore holes. This'll make money for someone, you'll see. There's a wrecked motor boat rotting in the corner next to a line of mobile cranes. The sky is incredibly blue, the air chill. There's ice on the surface ponds, scattered along the road sides like glass. Derek smokes slowly, black dog beside him. It's all gone to hell here, he says. I'd be better in Australia. Will you go? Too old.

In the East Dock Café, a Portakabin that's seen better days, I eat one of the best bacon sandwiches available in the whole of the east City. This place, heated by bottled gas and with a door that you have to kick to open, is known locally as Mossi's. Its founder, Modestino Cucciniello, came here from Italy after the war to seek his fortune and found it among black pudding breakfasts, bowls of beans and plates of egg. His daughter, Rosemary, large and endlessly smiling, cooks now. Her clientele all wear metal capped boots and luminous overalls. They have 8-high stacks of buttered-bread served without asking. The walls are strengthened with hardboard infills and 60s Formica. No graffiti. No cigarette machine. No music. Daily Mirror on the long bench. Tea that stains your teeth.

Through Mossi's grease-smeared windows you can see across the road to the flapping plastic scaffold cover of the almost completed City Wharf apartments. Here next? Bound to be[23]. Will Mossi's become a wine bar? Unlikely.

At the reception to launch the new David Mclean Group build I'm given the badge of Bill Addy, their Business Development Director.

His name crossed out and mine put in. He didn't show. I did. The place is full of suits, yellow ties, blue shirts, women who rush and gush. Punters? No. This is a jolly. The Sabina Turvey Jazz Trio play so quietly in the corner that it's quite possible they are miming. The canapés and champagne are expensive and extensive. On the walls, amid the wall hangings and large ceramics, are company slogans. View a life less ordinary. An address to impress. Art without label. Culture by association. I peer through the high windows looking for Mossi's but all I can see in that direction are stacked bags of Glascofoam insulation and the backs of expensive cars. Graham, a bright sales executive from Manchester, tells me the development is unique. Not a single apartment without a curving wall. £300,000 for a 30 foot living room and a bird's eye of pasteurised dock. Water does it. Essential 21st century. That's the reality of Cardiff, I tell him. This is the city that floats. He looks blank. Do you think your proximity to the prison will affect sales? Cardiff Gaol is a few hundred yards north, across the rail line. He doesn't answer.

In the corner a man in a bomber jacket is working his way furiously through the canapés. What's your connection with all this, I ask. None at all, he says. I'm the chairman's driver, brought him here from the airport. I couldn't live in a place like this. No air, no space. He swallows an olive, bites into a sort of Japanese pancake full of cheese and tied with a bunch of chives. No hills. I like hills. We look out across the very flat water.

Before City Wharf arrived this was car park. Before that Way's scrap yard, last resting place for Cardiff's trolley buses. Some are rumoured to be still here, under the dock water, their maroon sides dissolving just below the surface. Pre-war this was Taff Vale railtrack and signal box. A Victorian water fountain on the quayside. The Clarence, Stuart and York warehouses running beyond. Earlier it was salt marsh. Wading birds. Tides. Gullies. Fishermen. Before them tropical sea that came in as far as Storey Arms. Ever shifting space. A geological feng shui that's still in play.

WALKING OUT OF BUTETOWN

Before the city where did the waters reach? Most everywhere. Cairdife on its slump of pudding stone. Cardiff bounded by moor, salt meadow, tide field, estuary, and sinking soil. Before the sea walls were raised the spring tides brought salt water as far as the bottom of St Mary Street and drowned the car parks of MFI and Castle Bingo along Newport Road. This was a pond, this place. Water in runs and troughs. And the wind bringing in precipitation, as it still does, in dark enveloping clouds from the Atlantic, from the south west. I'm in Mount Stuart Square, solid Victorian, once home of shipping companies, coal traders and merchant banks. Over the past one hundred and fifty years, as Cardiff slowly moved from industrial powerhouse to post-modern mall, the Square and its occupants have changed. Gone is nineteenth century commerce. Gone too twentieth century grit, dabble and decline. In their place are twenty-first century liberal arts – broadcasters, bars, media companies. The WDA's new incubator at Beynon House. New apartments. Curves and style. At their centre the monolithic Coal Exchange – once vibrant with top-hatted traders selling options in not-yet-cut Aberdare steam coal – now home to concerts by Captain Paranoid and the Delusions, Roger McGuinn, Van Morrison, and Otis Grand.

Before Bute built his great docks, and well before the Exchange went up in 1884, this patch of land was little more than a sandbank, ringed with high tide driftwood and the site of Guest's Glass Works. Bottles, cups, jars. Window glass for the Empire well to do and the expanding American market. The smoking towers were used by arriving vessels as a beacon. The pits Guest had dug went nine metres down into sticky clay subsoil before they hit anything solid.

Bute Town was Soudrey – Sowdrie, Southrew, Sawdry, Sutton – the South Town. Orthography was imperfect, you spelled the place as you thought it sounded. There were saw mills and a sea-washed track running from the sea to the town's South Gate. You could fish. Pollution hadn't begun. The tides were full of great white horses. The moorland was ponded and thick with reed grass. The Taff, meandering without restraint, held fishing henges and beaten-earth slip ways from which coracles were launched. This was a tiny place. If you lived here you weren't much. If you were anything you didn't come here at all.

I'm walking where the dry route used to be. Bute Street, known

first as Bute Road down here
and as Lewis Street at its
northernmost extremity. It's
littered with well meaning
street art and traffic calming
chicanes. Where the paving
slopes buggy-friendly towards
the tarmac locals have beached
their Vauxhalls. The shrub
plantings beyond the rail
station are full of blown plastic
and fast food waste. My plan is
to follow where the hard earth

used to be until I reach real dry land. I'm ley walking. Leys are
straight tracks channelling power from ancient site to ancient site.
They network the globe. Where they intersect there's sway and
magic. The cosmic power they carry keeps the planet alive. Alfred
Watkins discovered these alignments in 1921 and wrote up his
theories in *The Old Straight Track*. Welsh necromancy. The ancient
routes of celtic power. But in the city they get lost. Where they
encounter industrial hard-core, excavation, canal, culverted river and
other man-made despoliation the leys alter. Their energy blackens,
becomes dissipated. They bend, they sink. Soured leys broken across
the Dumballs. St Mary's to the submerged iron-age sea harbour, no
longer visible. St John's to the Great Reen, sunk. The Longcross to
the Ely's tidal limits, twisted beyond recognition. But I'm going back
before this vandalism. I'm tracking where they used to flow.

Along Mermaid Quay the Faber novelist and Museum Director,
J.O. Jones, once celebrated his love of writing by arranging for the
now demolished Maritime Museum to mount poetry readings. The
late John Ormond, film maker and Oxford University Press bard,
read his Renoir Blue in the main gallery here. Blue water, blue slate,
blue graves, blue lazurite, blue slipper-clay, blue anything, blue
everything, blue everywhere. A swaying critic, full of Big Windsor
beer, stomped and heckled. Trouble with you, Ormond, you don't
engage with the people. What do they know about lazurite Renoir?
What do they care? The crowd, no one local, all imports from the city
two miles north, stood in edgy silence. What next? Would the poet
flatten his staggering accuser? Ormond coughed, looked about, held

his hand characteristically to his bad ear, straining to listen, heard, acted as if he had not. The poems continued. The complainer gave up. Through the Museum's great windows the mud-flatted Bay whirled with birds.

The world rarely really changes. Today, in the Ship and Pilot, Darren, or someone with a name like that, tells me he's not out to waste his useful time talking to Muppets. He knows I'm not from round here. This is a small community. Everyone knows everyone else. I'm from Lisvane. No. Well your from th apaartmunts then. You should be drinkin in Bar38[24] norere. This aint the Bay. It is not. I buy him a drink, no use falling out over nothing, dangerous in deep Butetown, whatever the night. He has a double Southern Comfort and Coke with a whiskey chaser. I don't take my notepad out. The Bay is two communities existing in the same space-time continuum. They pass through each other as they move. They rarely interact.

NORTH FROM THE OVAL BASIN

Heading north I skirt the Oval Basin, once the sea entrance to the Bute East Dock and later home to *The Sea Alarm*, preserved museum relic, cut for scrap in 1999 by three men with thermal lances working behind screens so the innocent, protesting public would not see. The original plan was to rebuild the Maritime Museum elsewhere and keep the collection intact. Where? Swansea. No one was sure. While we waited the treasures would be stored in rail sidings at Treforest. They would be put in packing cases in rented warehouses. They would be stored in converted bomb-storage tunnels at the Royal Navy Armaments Depot, Trecwn. They'd be sent to the moon. They'd be okay. They are the cream of Wales's now fast reducing industrial heritage. Sourced and restored at great cost. Some scrap yard in Newport got the remains of *The Sea Alarm*. I've no idea who got the rest.

The Basin is now decked with slatted hardwood and open for public use as a playground. You get food fairs here, tented exhibitions of prime Welsh beef burgers, Caws Llangloffan Farmhouse, Llanerch Cariad Dry White Wine, Rice Pudding from Llangadog, clog dancers for authenticity. As I pass the place is full of rally cars, the sun bouncing off their over-waxed surfaces, photographers nuzzling them like hungry sheep.

On the west side of the Basin stands Stefan Gec's *Deep Navigation*. Using bollards from the dock and disused rail from Tower Colliery the sculptor has cast two steel pillars at just over human scale. Resembling pit props the rusting sculptures have brass plates affixed to them. They bear the names of the ports to which coal had once been shipped from the West Bute and the names of the South Wales pits from which the black gold came. Risca. Wyllie. Bedwas Navigation. Hafodyrynys New Mine. Duffryn Rhondda. Garw. Rhigos No 7. Onllwyn No 1. Cwmgorse. New Drift Mine. Not that you need this information to appreciate the work. It explains itself.

I turn left here, skirt the snub-end of the filled-in West Dock, Bute's first, now covered with pale brick apartments. The docks once were the city. They might now be considerably diminished but the power of their flourishing is still around. It's in the shape of the roadways. It's in the soil below the paving. It's among the dock impedimenta – the bollards, anchor links, and steam-shovel jaws – which are fixed along the walkways like so many fairy lights. The ley line I'm following is sunk but flowing. I track it up.

Rather than walk through new housing I cross instead to the Bute East Dock. It remains in place, long and full of water, but with its access to the sea blocked. It's still serviced by the canal-like Bute Dock Feeder. This was dug in the early nineteenth century to bring water down from the Taff at Blackweir to fill the Docks and stop them silting up. The Bute East is empty: two swans, a slick of oil at the top end, dumped there by some local car-fixer, couldn't be arsed, the Ebden Hazler, the last barge on the water, roped as a bit of décor to the edge of Brain's new-build family pub, The Wharf. This dock once shifted ships like NCP processes cars. Forty-two acres of water servicing one thousand two hundred vessels annually. The stats we want to hear. It's leisure now. Chinese dragon races, a bit of power-boating, much fishing. The quay is lined with signs giving stern warnings against toxicity and algae which will bite into your face like an alien. Do not enter these waters. The fisherman I pass, tented and sat here for six hours already, has caught nothing, might soon, doesn't care. They're protecting themselves with those notices, he tells me. They always do. He's not concerned. We look out across the grey-green water. A gull lands like concord on floats. Diving duck scour the grubby bottom. There's a Sunny Delight bottle and a stack of burger casings. Some scaffold poles. A bike wheel. But mostly clear.

Bute, the second Marquess, John Crichton Stuart, only ever came here when he had to. His sprit, serge-suited, creases hot-ironed by his manservant, walks in front, gazes though thick eye-glasses across the blank water. Cardiff, so damp. He ran his empire by correspondence from his family seat, Mount Stuart, on the Isle of Bute. Dour and distant, afflicted with poor vision, ruthless, tireless. He bullied his estate managers and his agents into a precision of action of which Bill Gates would have been proud. It was he, more than his Catholic, romantic and utterly fantasist son, the third Marquess, who drew the marks on the map that turned Cardiff from slumbering backwater to exploding industrial force. By the mid-nineteenth century the town had become the world's largest coal-exporter. Forty years, that's all it took. Like Gates, Bute owned the entire operating system. There were no rivals to speak of. When one rose (such as Davies the Ocean and his docks at Barry) Bute simply made his own operation better. Bought up something. Put in a new rail access. Dug a new basin. Built a new wharf. He was irresistible. He owned everything. Early Cardiff maps with the Bute lands on them coloured red look like the world at the height of the British Empire. Bute, Celtic highlander, protestant, builder. A foreign founder. But now a fading wraith of mist along the wind-blown water. His names, and those of his descendants, permeate the city. Bute Park. Bute Esplanade. The Bute Dock pub. Bute Crescent. Bute Street. Bute Road. Bute Place. But just who was he? And who were his powerful family? Today, hardly anyone knows.

Along Lloyd George Avenue the warehouses have all been pulled down. The one that remains is being turned into The Granary flats. Enveloped. Nineteenth century stone outer, twenty-first century interiors. The sign outside says More Than Just Apartments. But someone last week painted out the *Just* and added a *No*. It read *No More Than Apartments*. The addition was removed within days.

My ley pushes itself through the top of the dock and into the space where St Paul's once stood. This was the religious heart of vanished Newtown, little Ireland, home of half of Bute's workers for one hundred and fifty years, bulldozed in a fit of self-righteous corporate slum clearance in the nineteen sixties. Here Bay turns to Adamsdown turns to Splott. Legendary working-class districts. Hot beds. Road calmed. Full of pubs and people on the street. Unvisited real Cardiff. Unless you happen to live here.

notes

1. Thomas Dadford snr, 1730-1809, canal engineer.
2. Described in more detail in The Town Walls on page 67.
3. See Briggs, John, *Before The Deluge*, Seren 2002 – an excellently priced plate size compendium of black and white Cardiff as it was before they built the barrage and drowned the Bay.
4. The Monument has been moved, lock stock, to a new plinth in the centre of Callaghan Square, south of the rail link. On it the Marquis still faces north, staring at the city and not the docks.
5. Designed by the call centre specialists, the Powell Dobson Partnership.
6. Graphic design at the BT IDC is by LifeWorks with text by Peter Finch.
7. The BT IDC has iris scanning and car number plate recognition, two independent National Grid power supplies and five back up generators with sufficient on-site reserves to power 30,000 homes for a week. There are no signs outside saying what the facility does.
8. In his hand he clutches a copy of Peter Meuiller's *Distaff* and the catalogue of book-bound objects showing at the European Centre for Traditional and Regional Culture at Llangollen, Clwyd. Childe Roland's paper book in a bottle, his bindings of torn paper, colours overlaid and rolling like waves, treaties with subject but no content, gestalt whiteness, French and welsh merging, fel melin, fel ymbarel, fel eli, fel melfa, fel tawel, fel dychwel, What are your plans for the future, my lord, Ham and Jam? There is light in these works; sometimes nothing but. Where else in this northern fastness can you find the word for light repeated so often that it glows. The friction of the signifier, the concrete base of Meuiller's brightness makes sparks in the Welsh air.
9. Bay of Fundy. New Brunswick. Nova Scotia. The New World. Whales. Hopewell Rocks. The Fundy National Park. Old Arcadian dikes. Highest tides in the world in the Minas Basin. 16 metres. No one has yet suggested blocking this basin. But let's wait.
10. Currently 1,500 people work at Cardiff County Hall.
11. *Building For Our Future: A White Paper on the Future of Cardiff. The Cardiff Debate*, Cardiff City Government, January, 2004.
12. Bute Docks Railway Co 1884 put in the junction but the pier was never completed.
13. WNO – Welsh National Opera – formed in 1943, Wales' internationally famous company.
14. CBDC – Cardiff Bay Development Corporation (1987-2000).
15. Crickhowell, Nicholas, *Opera House Lottery* (UWP 1997) p29.
16. Although it began life in the style of David Jones the lettering has actually ended up as a skewed Times Roman. Jonathan Adams' plan to "to break down the scale of the huge shell by using lines, words and individual letters" (J.Adams) remains nevertheless brilliantly intact.
17. The original and abandoned first plan for the slate's journey was slightly different. It was proposed that the foundation stone should travel by frigate, courtesy of the Royal Navy. Shouldn't be too difficult and would be vastly more prestigious. But a world emergency intervened. No ships were available.
18. "Cawn sglatys cynnes glytiau / crwst am wydd y croesty mau – We shall have slates warm slabs / as a crust on the timber of my house" – a couplet from the 15th century poet Guto'r Glyn.
19. Source: Welsh//Slate, suppliers of natural slate for architectural and roofing applications. Showroom in London. Vermont Green, Autumn Green, Mottled Purple, and Truthville Red, not used, are quarried in America.
20. Genuine enough – a section of the working Bute East Dock did bear this name.
21. In its time, during the second half of the nineteenth century, Cardiff was the greatest exporter of coal and steel in the world. In the 1880s 18% of total world exports of coal went out through Bute's coal staiths. By 1980 the West Dock had gone, the East Dock was closed, and exports were nil.

22. Cardiff and South Wales Wagon Works, Metropolitan Wagon Works. The coal had to be trucked in something.
23. The site has actually been developed as a showroom for VW cars.
24. Bar38 on Mermaid Quay has already been bought out and re-fitted. It's now Salt, and owned by Brains.

PENARTH
& THE COAST

THE TOWERS OF PENARTH

So is this Cardiff? At the book launch the scattering of Penarthians present are determined that it is not. Cardiff is over there. Beyond the headland, across the bay. This is the Vale. Back in the 80s there had been a move for change. Did Penarth want to join the City? Opinion went against. Someone clutches at my arm on the way out. Not everyone likes the Vale, you know. Cardiff's richer. They spend money there. Poor Penarth. Although it certainly doesn't look like that when you walk about.

Penarth is built across the great headland that protects Cardiff Bay from the prevailing storms. It's Victorian and largely unrecon-structed. Unlike central Cardiff where everything has either been knocked flat or altered beyond belief. Penarth stays largely as it origi-nally was. Brick, stone, bay windows, towers, turrets, porches, balconies, stained glass decoration, roof finials, crestings. Space, light.

Penarth wasn't actually much at all until the middle of the nineteenth century. A few farms – Pentwyn, Lancross, Kyming, Cwrt-y-vil, White Hall – and a cluster of cottages around the old parish church of St Augustine on the headland. Most of the land was owned by the Windsor family at St Fagans Castle. At best it gave an adequate return. But big money beckoned. In 1856 – inspired by the success of Bute at the mouth of the Taff – first the Ely tidal harbour was built and then Penarth Docks were dug. The venture[1] was to be a rival for Bute's all-embracing enterprise. Penarth enjoyed better access to deep water. There was no Cefn y Wrach shoal out there in

the estuary to avoid. The Docks were bought up by the principal carrier, the Taff Vale Railway, and success on a truly industrial scale followed. What went out through their new development? Iron ore, Rhondda coal.

Penarth above and beyond did what Cardiff did during this period. It mushroomed exponentially. Building took place in a great rush. Working class terraces were installed along the headland's northern face and a rash of eminently more desirable properties across its top. From nothing to everything in thirty years. The Windsor Estate laid the streets on spacious lines and encouraged speculative building. In co-operation with Bute they opened a toll road to Cardiff. They developed the sea front, straightened the shingle, built a sea wall and an esplanade, and encouraged the development of a pier. This was to be a genteel resort where Victorian perambulation could be practiced, sunbathing could be accommodated in shelters, and sea bathing considered if little carried out. Penarth was to be no industrial slum. In fact, much of its history since has been one of battle against the lumpen mass. As early as the 1880s complaints were being voiced about the visiting "ruffians from the hills" and their habit of outdoor eating, making noise, and drying their bathing clothes across the rocks. Later pubs would be closed and prostitutes hounded in an attempt to stop Docks' inhabitants living as docklanders always do. Despite its evident working class Penarth has never really been a refuge for the proletariat. It's ironic today, that for a place thick with retirees, youth and drugs have come back to haunt it. But there are worse places.

Tom Davies lives in The Towers, a converted coastguard lookout just off Marine Parade. The original three-storey tower was built in 1850 and an extension put on in 1955. The rocket house is now Tom's garage. They used to keep a lifeboat there and launch it to the sea along a gully at the back of Tower Hill Avenue. From his writing room on the top floor you can see from the Severn Bridge to Steep Holm. But the view is better when the trees in Windsor Gardens have lost their leaves.

For a novelist of the people and a former hellraiser of pop-music proportions Tom is surprisingly christian. With a small c. Can you have that? His conviction has long been present, since his time in Malaya in the early 60s. He had visions. St Augustine. Ginsberg seeing Blake in a bookstore. The troubles of the world in torrent. The problem, says Tom, is that there are victims. He kept a cap on the religion for enough years to earn himself a reputation as a sort of Oliver Reid for south Wales. They still talk of his three day parties in Peterstone where he had a large house near the Kinnocks. Did they turn out, I ask. Can't remember. The fugues can last a week. Evan Roberts gets them in Tom's *One Winter Of The Holy Spirit*.

Tom has written sixteen novels, including two best-sellers set in

Wales, and a bunch of books about pilgrimages (a mixture of St John of the Cross with Jack Kerouac) which go well both inside and outside the Christian community. He's 62 and doesn't stop (although he has given up his columns for the *Western Mail* and the *Liverpool Daily Post* as well as his weekly radio slot – life is getting short). Like many writers he does a solid morning in front of the monitor and then takes the afternoon out. Walking Penarth, café lunch, browsing the bookshop, buying fish food. I haven't been to Cardiff for at least nine months, he tells me. Don't need to. Everything is here. He's currently got three books on the go – none of them set in Penarth – but all of them involving himself. Fiction usually does that, circles back on you and your own experiences. *A Secret Life Of Polly Garter*[4] fantasises Dylan and Caitlin and how it might have been in Newquay. *A Child of the Times* is an hilarious biography of everyman. It started life as straight autobiography but then Tom's publisher told him that if he wanted it to sell then it would need to be about someone else. *A Lass Unparalleled* is, in Tom's opinion, his masterpiece. It's the story of a young Welsh writer who gets involved with a Shakespearean actress. Based on his own experiences, naturally, but he's not saying with whom.

We walk up Stanwell Road to towards the roundabout at the end of Windsor Road. The town's geographic centre. Tom is listing famous present day Penarthians. Linda Gail Lewis, Jerry Lee's sister, lives in the Marina. Dai Davies, David Bowie's one-time manager and discoverer of the Stranglers lives on Marine Parade. Weather girl Siân Lloyd. Pippa Davies, John Major's former advisor. Terry Hawkes. Peter Corrigan, the *Independent on Sunday*'s sports columnist. Rock and roll impresario Paul Barrett. Van Morrison? And after the unfair dismissal and sexual harassment court case which followed his album (the reviewed-as-dismal *You Win Again* with Jerry Lee's sister) certainly not. He's got a place in Pontcanna, hasn't he? No. We pass Turner House[4], James Pyke Thompson's 1888 shrine for his beloved painter, now home to Wales' Ffotogallery. And then Alun Michael's mansion, half hidden by hedge and as impressive with its tiles and large bay windows as a late Victorian house can be. It's got dirty windows, says Tom. And it has.

Penarth circles its central roundabout in a way that Cardiff never could. No threat of snarl or tailback. In Anne Hallett's Windsor Books there's only one Davies title on the shelves, *Through Fields of Gold*. I buy it and we theatrically get Tom to autograph it in front of the store's other two customers. Outside the sun fills the streets. There's space and a distinct lack of imminent violence. On the pavements people know each other. On the roads traffic is slow. In David Morgan's Penarth Patio, where I consume an inadequate ploughman's, we meet musician Danny Chang. He's a member of Tom's Penarth Revival group. Why does Penarth need reviving, I ask. The pair sit back and display knowing nods. The place is going downhill. We need to buy the pier, open an art house multi-screen, bring creative people back. Penarth is changing. Ah yes. Too many visiting ruffians, I expect.

But in reality the Esplanade does appear to all be in the hands of one man and there are suggestions that he might redevelop the pier as an aquarium. God help us, mutter the Penarth Revivalists. Already the Victorian baths have been converted to a pub and subsequently closed for lack of drinkers. Buddleia can now be seen growing from its blue lias walls. If something isn't done Kentucky Fried Chicken and arcades of gambling machines will move in. Seasides abhor a vacuum.

We turn through Glebe Street – Penarth's Chinese quarter, Tom calls it – and return to The Towers through Alexandra Park (aviary, Victorian clipped box, quince and forsythia). Tom is explaining that during his wild period he was simultaneously writing a column for the *Times*, fronting an arts programme on HTV (*Nails*) and running a coal business. Coal? Yes. Bagging and then re-selling it round town. It seemed a good idea at the time and actually made some money but then the miners went on strike. Tom has always been enterprising. A central plank of his philosophy is that if you write about violence or celebrate it in film then you get more real violence in return. His I, Conker[5], which details much of this theory, came out in 1994. It didn't sell well. Not wanting to let things lie Tom shipped in a bit of his own money, several thousand in fact, and spent it on promotion.

He took space in the national newspapers, full pages in Welsh magazines, employed journalist Herbert Williams to write taster pieces, sent out press releases, pushed his media contacts. Big time. How many copies did you sell in total? 200. Which proves the point, really. If it's going well then promote it hard and it'll do even better. If it's limping, then leave it alone.

We turn up into Marine Parade, a road of great houses, huge Victorian mansions set back in acres of garden, gates, arched porches, turrets. In the 1880s the ship-owners, the exporters and the coal owners who had started off in the big Cardiff dockland houses along Mount Stuart Square and Bute Crescent moved in, fleeing the working hoards. Penarth here has the feel of leafy suburb that's reached the top. Pontcanna is Cardiff's media wannabe. Aspirational, moving up. Penarth is the City's media made it. Serene. Except, of course, that it is not actually the City. Not really Welsh either. Nor multi-cultural. The name Penarth is about as upsettingly cymric as things get. Tom the Book[6] returns to the Towers to write some more. Late afternoon catch up. Holiday done.

PENARTH HEAD

Triassic, flaky red marls, tea green marls, narrow, unstable, pink and white alabaster, gypsum, calcium sulphate, adherent clay. This was once as flat the salt lakes of Namibia, hot as central Australia, sun up like an iron gun. The hand of something touching it but not the hand of man. Penarth Head – head of the bear[7] – is made of the flaky red stone you can see in Llandaf, in Radyr, quarried from the Taff side and built into much of the Cardiff structure. Here it's turning to a rain of dust as it erodes in the wind prevailing from the south west. You can listen to it fall from the face. A slow drizzle, rucking in rills around the cliff foot, drifted like construction aggregate.

Penarth Head is the two hundred foot high outcrop to the south west of Cardiff. It protects the Port which hides in its lee. St Augustine's Church[8] on top, with its distinctive saddle-back tower, has been a maritime marker on admiralty charts for hundreds of years. As they sailed up through storm and mist into Tiger Bay what would they see? St Augustine's to port, the cones of Guest's glass-works[9] to starboard. Aim between them into calm water. Tie up and get drunk.

If Penarth is anything then it's this headland. It's the town's historical origin, first farms here, first cluster of cottages, fields laid for wheat, for cattle and the rest for withy beds. St Augustine's on site with its stone carved cross since the thirteenth century. Marls falling into the bay for thousands of years.

The walk round at sea level passes the refurbished Penarth Custom House and Dock Offices, once the Penarth Head Inn, now Benigno Martinez's slick restaurants, El Puerto and La Marina. Maritime Cardiff is as busy as it has always been – dredgers incoming, dinghies, motor yachts, and power-engined inflatables exiting the Barrage into Cardiff Roads. Herring Gulls. Rooks. Lesser Black Backs. The beach is Rhaetic rock bed smashed, mixed with fragments of gun emplacement fallen from the cliff top, iron-stuffed ferro-concrete girders that once made up a searchlight installation, sections of cliff stairway, but miraculously free of plastic jetsam, scoured away by the raging tides. These are the Dardanelles, so called because of their one-time fortification, a dumping ground for builder's rubble and wrecks. Fishermen in full chest-waders catch cod, pollack and huss with rods as long as the poles from trolley buses. In the Channel a score of white-sailed dinghies cluster tightly round a marker-buoy waiting for the claxon that will mark the start of their race. Soon this low-tide treck will be replaced with an all-weather walkway[10] cantilevered to the stabilised cliff face and running from Cardiff Bay Barrage to Penarth Pier.

Victoriana meets Twenty-First Century leisure industrial. Shares in Rabiottis, Penarth's sea-front diner, will rise.

The Esplanade is where it all happens or nothing does. Gentle, windswept, ice cream, kids on scooters, old ladies with sticks. Walks with a face of air. Views of Somerset, Flat Holm, Steep Holm, buoys, boats, rocks and sludge.

The climb back is hardly breath wrenching. A zig-zag along the woodland walk in the grounds of the now municipal but once great house, the Kymin. On up Church Avenue to pass the St Augustine's grave of Joseph Parry with its white harp headstone. Then to gaze back suddenly at Cardiff in all its apparent hugeness. These are Mariners Heights, Padget Road, John Street where the sailors once lived but the new crachach now do. Sea-facing apartment developments are heavily signposted as Private Estate, No Public Access, we like the quiet and the sound of the sea, clear off, leave us alone. Headlands School occupies the former Taff Vale Railway's Penarth Hotel building. 1865. The Portway is down Dock Road, below it. MX5s double parked, blondes in sun-glasses, tan, no trainers. Slacks and mobiles. Blazers strolling into Martinez's up-market emporia for a steak and vodka-shot. Penarth as it likes to be.

A Liberal Version of the Penarth Sea Angling Club List of Penarth Pier Fish

Bass
Coalfish
Cod
Conger Eel
Dab
Dib
Dob

Dogfish
Darkfish
Doodlefish
Esplanade Knickers
Flounder
Fillet
Mullet
Mallet
Moosh
Plaice
Prick
Pollack
Plop
Poor Cod
Dreadful Wallop
Pouting
Spitting
Moaning
Whining
Getting Your Hair Off
Rocklings
Rollings
Silver Eel
Sausages
Soul
R&B
House
Handbag
Adrodd
Welsh Grey
Grecian 2000
Whiting

THE BILLY BANKS

I'm in the Bowery. I've come up Windsor Road from Cogan and turned left up High Street and I'm here. Docktown. Ten pubs. Lanes. Handrails. Cobbles. This is the Penarth they built for the Irish immigrants, for the coal tippers, the lifters and the shifters. Stone houses, sloping terraces. The Penarth that faces into the dark due north. There was as much drunken disorder here in the rollicking eighteen-sixties as in the whole of Butetown. Today, in the twenty-first century, it's quiet. Neighbours washing cars, two kids and their bikes, a dog walker. No one sweating. No one swearing. Dock Subway Road which once poured hundreds of men daily under the High Level TVR[11] sidings and onto the gritty dockside is gone. The road ripped up. The steps demolished. The subway filled. No docks either. Below me where once great ships smoked and coal gushed like grain are the silent sparkling yachts of the new Marina. Men in white trousers wearing navy blue captain's caps. Overweight women with gold handbags and matching shoes. Small dogs on long leads.

Penarth's Docks disappeared in time with Cardiff's. Penarth Haven, the eastern end, was used as landfill, and is now capped, straddled with maritime apartments, street art, glass and shine. To the west is Portway Marina and the locks which let the yachts slide slowly into the Bay. I'm on Paget Terrace[12] with the whole of the Marina and Cardiff Bay spread out before me. The new city landmarks are the Millennium Centre; the Assembly, still building; and St David's Hotel. They are all there. One of the best views in Cardiff and it's

Penarth's. John Osmond lives here. Journalist, author, political thinker and the only man I know who can fall asleep at the dinner table and still get invited back. We're going to walk to the Billy Banks – the Prince Charles flats – that piece of eastern Europe that runs right along the Penarth headland ridge. From Butetown they look like teeth in a giant jawbone. Close up like a suburb of Bucharest. Flats. No

lifts. Urine stairwells. Irvine
Welsh country. Have you read
him, John? Not yet.
    For a man who spends a
good deal of his time hanging
around with poets John is a
considerably political animal.
His great-grandfather ran a
hauliers shifting stone from the
quarries at Culverhouse Cross.
They lived at Great House,
Ely. Moved there from the
west country. There's a photo

of some of their workers in a steam-powered lorry on John's landing
wall. E. Osmond and Sons[13]. Shirtsleeves. Weathered faces leaning
from a glass-less cab window. These origins are important. John in a
suit always looks uneasy. You get the feeling he'd prefer to be out of
doors somewhere shovelling earth or cutting wood.
    John's books mostly circle the same subject: devolution. *Wales
apart. Wales on its own. The Centralist Enemy. Creative Conflict. The
Divided Kingdom. Welsh Europeans. A Parliament for Wales*[14]. When you
have a good idea then keep it going. On his study wall is a framed
letter from fellow-Penarthian, Saunders Lewis, congratulating him on
the arguments proposed in *The Centralist Enemy*. The great and the
good recognised Osmond's strengths early on. His background is
journalism. When, in the sixties, he was offered two jobs simultaneously – working for the Press Association at the House of Commons
in London or hacking as political correspondent for the Cardiff
Western Mail – he found choosing easy. This was the pivotal moment,
he tells me. Do I become a Brit, take the big one, and move to
London, or follow my heart and remain Welsh? He chose to stay local.
    After a bruising campaign in support of devolution during the 70s
he launched the fortnightly political and cultural journal, *Arcade*.
That kept him quiet until the magazine failed in 1982. For the next
fifteen years he was first a journalist for HTV, then an independent
TV director, and finally deputy editor on the early broadsheet and
quite readable *Wales On Sunday*. But nothing ever really worked for
long. There were periods of drinking, periods of holding the head in
the hands. Everything I touch gets defeated, he once told Leo Abse.

But it is from your defeats you learn, was the reply.

And he did, too. He set up the networking organisation, the St David's Forum, in the late 80s and became Director of the public policy research think tank, the Institute of Welsh Affairs, after that. Shirts, ties, haircuts, interviews on television. A chairman to chide and guide him. More books. Research reports. A quarterly magazine, *Agenda*, which told the world what Wales was doing. The devolution highway. High-profile dinners. Interventions. Consultations. None of which stopped him continuing to consort with creative writers. At Welsh Union of Writers conferences and Academi functions John can always be relied upon to either cavort or collapse or both.

The Billy Banks flow west from Paget Terrace in an almost pristine sixties line. They have that mid-century failed social solution look about them. District heating stacks. Communal grass. Balconies. Grey pebble dash. Connecting walls perforated by chequer-board laid bricks. Today the flats themselves have largely been abandoned. There are hundreds of them, named after a curious mix of Welsh and English royalty – Prince Charles Court, Prince Llywelyn Flats, Prince Rhodri House. The windows are boarded with ventilated metal, the doors blocked and broken. Crap in the courtyards. Aluminium bell and intercom plates belted by stones, dented out of their recesses. In their time the blocks won prizes for their architecture. They also suffered the standard sink estate disasters of asbestos, damp, leaking water systems, and being belted out of shape just for the fun of it vandalism. They became a ghetto for the municipal dumping of problem families. Punk music like an electric saw day and night. Dope in the flowerbeds.

Most of the residents have been moved on apart from the fifteen or so who bought under the right to purchase and remain. Spectres in a disused land. We pass a washing line of black tee shirts strung across overgrown shrubbery. Heavy metal amid the broken bricks.

Below us in a steep hillside of grass and bush are abandoned cars. Wrecks crashed and burned when the flats were full. Glue-powered head bangers hurtling their stolen Astras in an arc of noise and flame. Nature reclaims them. They rust. Grass grows through their frames.

This whole area was once quarry – five separate gulches dug for limestone. The spoil was tipped down the hillside by tramway into heaps – *banks* as they were known. Beyond them lay the Taff Vale Railway coal yards – officially the Williams Sidings. The Bowery kids clambered the banks, the Billy Banks. All swept away when the flats were developed. And soon the flats themselves. According to John they'll shortly be demolished and the site marketed as Penarth Heights. Apartments. Marina View. Sea Vista. Bay Boulevard. Exclusive. Certainly.

With his daughter, Morwenna, high on his shoulders John and I track down through the mud and slip to Terra Nova Way. Edge of the Marina. The speed-humped Penarth Portway. New terraces. Slim and bright painted. Like Tenby. Barbeques smoke on the brick patios. Passion fruit climb around glass doorways. Clean and bright but not really built for endurance. Where will all this be in twenty years, asks John, pointing at the nineties-style Barretesque arrivals. Are they going to stay the course? Morwenna couldn't care less. She pulls at her father's hair. Behind and above us is the Bowery. No one calls it that now. The residents are all too civilised. History amended. Penarth is Penarth. No districts. I can see the Assembly from my window, announces John. Do you go there often, I ask, imagining him arriving at work by Bay traversing boat or by walking along the Barrage. Hardly ever, he says. I get the information I need from the internet. But for a devolutionist, it's nice to look at the place, nonetheless.

WASHINGTON

In the municipal cemetery abutting the golf course at the bottom of Lavernock Road we find him. Saunders. Yma Y Gorwedd Saunders Lewis 1893-1985. Santaidd Fair Fam Duw Gweddia drosom. Mary, Mother of God, Look over us. Founder of Plaid Cymru. Playwright, poet, critic, nationalist. Nobel nominee. Catholic. Red neck. His slate gravestone[15] is larger than everyone else's by about twelve inches. In

his day he was the most celebrated Welsh writer alive. Today his reputation wavers. Anti-Semite. Like anti-Black. Just can't be done. No flowers, or sign of them. Morgan Francis, teacher, poet, boat-builder, fitter's mate, and angel maker, has brought me here to somehow locate Penarth's Welshness. Hard to do. Every other stone is in English. As grey as the clouds. A grave-digging machine slows our exit. No sun.

We're on the way to the Washington Gallery[16] for Molly Parkin's new show. Parkin: 60s fashion icon, writer, style guru, fashion editor for *Nova*, *Harper's* and *The Sunday Times*. She was famous for her excesses, her marriages, her affairs, for blacking out on stage in an alcoholic stupor, for commandeering New York's Chelsea Hotel, falling over, standing up, famous for being famous. And for art. Writer, painter. Blocked for twenty years, the juice was once again flowing. We were promised large canvases, spirituality, Celtic inspired expressionist smear and splash.

En-route we divert via the great houses of Marine Parade looking for finials. Morgan reckons someone here has replicas of the dragon atop City Hall done in red pantile on the ridge of their roof. We don't find them. Taken down, nicked, claims Morgan, knocked off and sold. Cheapskates. The dragon with one wing we spot on the top of Ty Llwyd in Bridgeman Road is a *griffin* the owner insists. Is there a difference? Certainly. Dragons are Welsh. Griffins are not.

The Washington Gallery is in the converted half of the wonderfully art deco Washington Cinema on the corner of Stanwell Road and Herbert Terrace. When radio was king the talkies showed here. Now TV has turned the world to dust the round-fronted entrance is a gallery. The auditorium, the other half, is a down-market branch of Hyper-Value. On Stanwell Road you can buy critical comment, cappuccino, *Art Monthly*, *Poetry Wales*. In Herbert Terrace there are wrestling videos, luminous green shower mats and repro ceramic bed pans for hanging on aspirational lounge walls. In the window is a complete inflate-it-yourself bouncy castle, a canvas gazebo and a huge tub of one pound bulb planters. Near the cash desk is a pyramid of tinned east-European beans.

The Gallery is run by Australian former-journalist Maggie Knight. The place is her vision and her labour, saved from development as a car park in 1996, revived from being a bingo hall, made new. The space has been turned into a not-for-profit Conran-styled café, shop, Gallery and community space. The whole of Penarth can be proud of this. Retirement banished. Culture with gun in hand. Anything like it in the city? No.

The Parkin private view is packed. The paintings are luminous, large, full of life. The Celtic connection is hard to get but Molly insists it's there. I did most of these this year, she tells me. A couple of months hard painting. There are more than sixty canvases here. She's faster than Andy Warhol, and he had a factory. The show is thick with art liggers. Lesbian shorthairs, Japanese students, wig wearers. Orange trousers, pink shirt and bow-tie, sex change. Sophisticated Indians, academics with leather elbow patches, bank clerks. An unshaven in a donkey jacket, a retired grey-head in a collar-less suit and green boots, masses of jewellery. Big knits, snapper dappers. Make it up. Your are what you want. This is where bohemia has gone. Molly's big paintings, her *Up The Mountain* oils are numbered in sequence and are offered for a thousand or so. The red dots are starting to form and by the end of the show's run have covered everything. The process works.

Behind his wine glass Ifor Davies, art historian and a contender as Wales' top painter, tells me that he thinks of Penarth as a sort of Opidum, a pre-Christian hillfort rebuilt. St Augustine's church on top, the town clustering in supplication to its sides. Penarth as Greece or Italy. Slow. Full of art. Full of sun.

The crowd noise increases. Molly, dressed in her trade-mark pre-raphaelite bat costume and primary-coloured head binder, circles her guests. I have a conversation, of which later I can remember nothing, with the feminist historian Deirdre Beddoe. We shook hands so it must have been positive. On behalf of the gallery Prof Stephen Knight welcomes the world. We drink some more. This is a Molly Parkin show. That's what you do. We expect outrage somewhere along the line. But we're too old. The moment has passed. There is none.

LAVERNOCK

Klimaschewski has put the car into neutral and pulled the hand-brake. Marconi[17], he says with full Slavic pomp and ignorance, was Polish. His name, Markoni. It's obvious. We're at the sea end of the road to Lavernock point, where the farm is, and the mud. Klim, Witold Jozef Winawa Klimaschewski, Count of Poland, filmmaker, author, deluded modernist, is given to the permanent enhancement of his father's country. He's part of the Cardiff Polish diaspora who see their task as the remaking of a Poland of the mind. The world will know again of the might of the white eagle. The dismembered nation will once more be made a dynamic whole. There will be horses on the streets and cavalrymen with swords. They will drink their large vodkas with single gulps and ride proud in the city squares. You shee, Peter. His accent is thick because he's thinking about it. Thish little country of yoursh ish nothing when you compare it to the might of mine. But isn't Poland overrun by Russians, I ask, innocently? The sun glints on the battered Jaguar's bonnet. We will open the wine, says Klim, accent dropping, avoidance technique, reaching into the glove. There is a bottle here which I stored for reference. He pushes the cork of the Sauternes down the neck with a pen. We drink and look out over the grey Jurassic limestone at the dirty sea.

These are the seventies and Lavernock still holds sway, just, as the nearest place to Cardiff, if you exclude prim Penarth, where the sea can be broached. It's free, there's nothing to buy. The nearest pub, the Golden Hind, around the headland, won't let you in unless you are a

holiday park member. The scrub and unimproved meadow of the cliff tops are dotted with 50s caravans. Lounging beside them are men in rolled-up cavalry twill trousers and open-necked shirts. In the channel is a tanker, heading for the docks at Barry to unload. Klim identifies it as a Polish merchantman. The mighty fleet, you shee. They shail even here to your misher-able Barry. Shall we get out and walk, I suggest? Walk, ah no. We will consume this nectar and take the sun through the windscreen. Two girls in shorts, carrying a bag of towels and a beach-ball pass us, heading for the rocks. Klim smiles and waves his bottle of Sauterne. Mungo Jerry's 'In The Summertime' rolls from the radio. Klim is ignored.

Thirty years later the farm has gone, replaced by Lavernock House, a new build, garage, mowed lawns. Guglielmo Marconi, the first man to send a voice message by wireless, sat here in 1897 and spoke to his assistant George Kemp on Flat Holm out in the Channel. There's a celebratory plaque on the wall of the Church of St Lawrence put there in by the local rotary in 1947. A Welsh first from an Italian Irishman speaking to a island-stranded Englishman. Radio enthusiasts come here to stare and wonder. Flat Holm is so near that Guglielmo could have got his message to George by shouting.

The route to the beach used to be by rail to Lavernock Station (closed by Beaching as utterly unprofitable in 1968) and then a long haul down Cosmeston Road with pushchairs, bags of sandwiches, flasks of tea. Today you can drive to the car park back of the church or walk here on the coast path up from Penarth. There's a water pump station like a small fort in the bushes near Ranny Bay then the splendour of the limestone pavements, the marls and the best Rhaetic beds anywhere in Britain. We cross them in late March, strong, low sun, the flat rocks fractured like mortared paving. This is Cardiff's foreshore. More visitors in 1930 than Barry. Almost deserted now. A Victorian sewage outlet pipe concreted to the sea, mortar and stone chippings ladled over it like ice cream. On the cliff top the Marconi Holiday Village trailer park is protected by the remains of a string of World War Two gun batteries, barracks, ammunition storage lockers, radar stations and searchlight houses. Wrecked but, somehow, not defeated. Adder's tongue fern and cowslip grow among them.

The limestone beds turn into sand at St Mary's Well Bay and it's a steep climb between army rust and sewage leak to the cliff top and the path back. The barbed-wire topped wire weave fences of the caravan park have been repaired and re-knitted like darned socks. At the padlocked entry gate a warning notice announces that ACTION WILL BE TAKEN AGAINST ANYONE PROPPING OPEN THIS ENTRY SYSTEM. But who would want to go in? Behind it is a brick hut which someone has tried to burn out and a heap of brick rubble. Cans litter the bushes. Fun. In the summertime. But it's still spring and no one's about.

The slow return path up across Sutton Farm to the Cosmeston Road feels like Poland must have done in 1945. Decay, bust reinforced-concrete, fences you can't breach, slices of your land taken by others. Klim died of a heart-attack in the 1980s but I can still hear his voice. You will drink, Peter? Hedgerows full of birdsong.

SULLY'S TERMINAL BEACH

This is Ballard's spiritual landscape – *Terminal Beach*'s dark Welsh twin. The Cessna overhead, the deserted hospital, the marginal Triassic, the coiled razor wire and the security cameras of the naval base. Silence. Cardiff subtopia. Water, sand, concrete, crystal. The sea our corporate memory, thick with effluent, flotsam and oil. This is the coastal path from Sully Island to Bendrick Rock. It tracks the edge of dormitory suburbia, the margin between flash-flood siltstone and the vast Vopak chemgas storage inland. We edge along it, past wire-mesh and rusted doorway. Sites overgrown with grass, derelict, deserted. Evidence of camp fire. Rash of dumped hard-core. Dandelion, cocks-foot, ryegrass. On the beach in the sun-powered chill someone has built an enclosure of loose rock and jetsam. The fire in its centre is shielded from the wind by a fridge door strung to a hunk of tree limb. A rope holds a primitive pot, heating. Mad Max. The family in occupation stare at me with blank faces. I wave but nothing registers.

Beyond is the sea face of Ty Hafan, children's hospice, built like a beached liner. Porthole windows, white, flag masts, trimmed lawn. One Nissan in the car park. An adult face moving slowly inside a

curtained room. A bright coloured kids playground. Empty. The patients stay, they don't leave. The walls are full of light.

The path slips through Alder and Beech wood, Hayes Point, abandoned tyres on the shoreline. Sully Hospital stands empty in its huge grounds, v-shaped footprint, modernist, the past's idea of the future. Italian cypress, smoke bush, the wreck of a child's garden rocking horse. A sign on the decayed mesh fence warns of guard dogs and patrols but like the rest of the coast no one is about. The sanatorium was built for tuberculosis sufferers in 1932 by William Pite, Son and Fairweather. Its white masonry frame supports large expanses of full-height glass, south facing to collect air and sun. There were Home Office moves in 2002, later abandoned, to house 750 asylum seekers here. Young men. They could have sea fished. Watched the tankers on the road into the Windmill Industrial estate. Hiked into Sully to visit the sub post-office, the church or hunt vainly for the vanished castle. Some of the hospital's top windows have been smashed by stone throwers, wet rot is attacking the doorways. But the white is still largely unblemished.

As the path bends around Bendrick Rock, marked by the WI Millennium Plaque at Sully Yacht Club as site of dinosaur footprints, HMS Cambria's security cameras catch us face on. This is a land-base for the Royal Naval Reserve, grounds as neat as 1939, but today deserted. The coiled wire top of ferro-concrete posts shows at least three styles – razor wire, hanging barbs, four-point twirls[18]. There's no flag on the post. No guns. No boats. A seaward path descends to the Triassic. The top layers are half covered with tar, hard-topped like desert roadways. Below, somewhere, in the Mercia mudstone, the tracks of a Norian three-toed theropod. Large as your hand, walked here when this was desert, no one around then either.

Cyril Hodges[19] approved of J.G. Ballard. He was someone I should have got to write for the magazine I ran but I never did. I think I admired Ballard's work far too much to actually have to deal with it.

It was better distant. Cyril, however, was close – an industrialist, fervent nationalist and supporter of the arts who lived in Smithies Avenue. Heart of slow, sun-facing Sully. He'd cycled every road in Wales, he claimed, but I think he exaggerated. He was there in the tiny audience at the first ever No Walls Poetry reading given by myself, David Callard and Geraint Jarman at the Boucher Hall in 1965. Round-faced, smiling, slow spoken, undemonstrative. He'd clap your back, shake your hand, tell you you were doing well, even if you weren't. What he wanted most of all was to see someone push Wales on in the new literary world. Dylan and his ghost kept us old. We all spoke with the voice of Caradoc Evans. So the world thought. Wales was a literary museum. Cardiff was full of smog and smoke. There was coal in the streets. Land of Lascars and lying Taffs. Cyril knew we had to move on.

His device was *Second Aeon*, my avant-garde Cardiff-based literary magazine, full of European translation, beat America, Welsh outsider, concrete poetry and other outrage. He'd show up at my Maplewood Court flat, creative base, editorial office, and home, and leave envelopes of cash on the mat. Not a word in them. Just stacks of fivers. £300, £500. When I'd ring him he'd say you know what to do with it. Spend it on making the magazine bigger. Print more. Stay solvent. Who would you like to see in there, I'd ask? Not for me to say. You're the editor. Spend it well. I did. The pattern, punctuated by the occasional celebratory meal and the odd drive through the Sully streets, continued until Cyril's untimely death in 1974.

At high speed the causeway to Sully Island covers with incoming tide. Warning notices at each end explain your plight. Get caught and you'll be charged. At the eastern point of the island is evidence of an iron age camp, blasted by practising guns during the war, trench, two-metre rampart, worn. West point is clustered with sea fishermen. In the 1970s the owner of Avalon, ladies leisure, health and beauty centre, put in a planning application to build a subterranean branch on the island's centre. It was rejected. If it hadn't been there would now be a hard-top above the tide race. Four-wheel drives, Mercs, VW beetles with flower vases on the dash. The sea foams, flows. The fishermen, returned to the main land, drink tea at the Bistro Bar, a shoreside hut set a causeway's end like a customs post. Talk is of cod, whiting, pouting and the odd strap-conger. Someone caught a thorn-back ray last summer. They wear NATO camouflage coats, wool hats, dark glasses. Rockabilly leaks from a radio. Could be America. Ballard would make them hospital security guards on break. Alienated Londoners. But most of them work locally, bus drivers, fitters, live in Penarth, or Cadoxton or Barry. Behind is the Captain's Wife pub, built on the site of the old farm. Then the racked caravans – Cameo 32x10, The Vogue, Avon, Atlas, Chardonnay, The Granada – names in Olde English script. Inside you expect to find Midlands' residents eating chicken in the basket and drinking Blue Nun.

Do you think this is Cardiff? I ask my companion. Reviewing what I've written, in a pub in some other part of Cardiff. Well. Her answer takes as long arriving as one of Cyril's would. In a sense. Yes. Suburbs go on, don't they. They do. But Cardiff's finish here. Terminal Beach. Nothing beyond.

notes

1. Early investors included Crawshay Bailey, Thomas Powell, John Nixon, James Insole, the Hon Windsor Clive, the Rev. George Thomas, W.S Cartwright and others.
2. Bono of U2 claims that reading Tom's *Merlyn the Magician and the Pacific Coast Highway* changed his life.
3. The other volumes are *One Winter Of The Holy Spirit, Fire In The Bay* and *Black Sunlight*
4. Turner House was built on land previously occupied by Taylor's Farm. The Gallery is managed by the National Museum of Wales.
5. *I, Conker*, Gwasg Gomer, 1994. More of Tom's theories are in *The Man of Lawlessness: The Media, Violence and Prophecy*, Hodder & Stoughton, 1989
6. Tom the Book was Tom's nickname when he lived in Maerdy while working on his mining community novel, *Black Sunlight*, Macdonald, 1986
7. Or head of the ridge, take your pick.
8. The tower of first St Augustine's was less impressive but it was a tower nonetheless. The present structure, on the same site, was designed by William Butterfield and completed in 1866
9. At what is now Mount Stuart Square
10. The present plan is not the first. Edwardian entrepreneurs talked of building a tram link from the pier around the headland to the dock with its rail station and a foot tunnel under the Ely to the Ferry Road peninsular. The foot tunnel was built but for the use of

Grangetown residents working at Penarth Docks.

11. TVR – Taff Vale Railway

12. Paget Terrace was formerly known as Dock Road. It led directly to the quays. In the 1880s the Earl of Plymouth, Robert George Windsor Clive, who owned most of Penarth, married Alberta Paget. Dock Road was renamed in her honour.

13. Named after John's grandmother, Elizabeth.

14. *The Centralist Enemy*, Christopher Davies, 1974; *Creative Conflict*, Routledge, 1978; *The Divided Kingdom*, Constable, 1988; *Welsh Europeans*, Seren, 1997; *A Parliament for Wales*, Gomer, 1994.

15. Carved by Jonah Jones

16. The Washington Galley runs classes, shows, readings and other cultural events in the heart of Penarth. Check its excellent web site at www.washgallery.com

17. Guglielmo Marconi, born Bologna, Italy, 1874, the second son of Giuseppe Marconi, an Italian country gentleman, and Annie Jameson, daughter of Andrew Jameson of Daphne Castle in the County Wexford, Ireland. Never visited Poland.

18. *A Brief History of the Invention & Development of Barbed Wire* can be found at www.barbwire-museum.com/barbedwirehistory.htm. There are more than 530 patented barbed wires, with approximately 2,000 variations. Collectors are often eccentrics.

19. Cyril Hodges (1915-1974) – pen-name of Cyril Hughes – who wrote *Seeing Voice, Welsh Heart* (1965), Galerie Karl Flinker, *Coming of Age* (1971), JJC Ltd, and *Remittances* (1971), Second Aeon.

BEYOND

NEWPORT ISN'T CARDIFF

Newport isn't Cardiff. Barely eight miles separate the outer suburbs of these two south Wales conurbations. But that eight could be eight million. Essentially they are the same sort of places – coal ports built on estuaries; towns around river crossings – Cardiff on the Taff, Newport on the Usk. Both are lapped by the high-tidal dinginess of the mighty Severn. In the early nineteenth century Newport's exports outstripped Cardiff's by two to one. The town itself was bigger, smouldering around its castle, fed by its canals, waiting for Brunel's railway to come. But this early leadership was not to be sustained. By 1851 Cardiff was on a roll, outstripping everywhere else in Wales, and for a brief time, the Western world. Cardiff, Welsh industrial epicentre, city, capital. Newport, although it grew and continued to grow, never quite recovered its early eminence. The rivalry between the two cities is defined by a sort of mutual ignorance. There is scant interaction between the two places. Little exchange of shopping traffic. Few split families. Newport largely ignores Cardiff's gleaming entertainment complexes. Cardiff rarely shops at John Frost Square. Cardiff's notorious Soul Crew of soccer hooligans draws its membership from as far away as Merthyr, Bridgend and even Llanelli. But never Newport. There is an impenetrable fog between these two places. Put an international border post at Castleton, the village halfway between on the old road, and no one would notice.

The bus I'm catching is timed to reach the Royal Oak at 8.02 but it's early because the Millennium Stadium F.A. Cup playoffs have

blocked Cardiff city centre to all traffic. The buses start further out. Cardiff has been convinced it loves football. How they doing? The question plied by barbers, milkmen, bakers, street traders, bus conductors and paper-sellers down the decades. They mean the soccer: the Blues, Ninian Park, the City. Cars have been arriving from out of town all day. Streaming down Newport Road with colours flying from their rear windows. Pennants on their aerials. Painted faces, cans of Castlemaine, tattoos in the back. With a lifetime disinterest in football behind me I'm glad to be going somewhere else. I haven't been on a bus in an age and not on this route for thirty years. The project is to sample the history of Cardiff's rival in the company of someone who lives there, my canal walking companion, John Briggs. Take the bus, he advised, use the experience. You can see the world from the upper deck. It's evening but the sky is bright. At the stop there are two girls with college packs, gum and Bensons. A man with a terrier. A fat black woman, coughing, towing a shopping trolley. When the green 30 comes they all get on first even though I was here before them. Experience tells.

The bus driver recognises me. On the entire fleet there's only one man I know and this is he. A writer, an Iranian William McGonagall, known through much of the south east for his rhyming couplets and ready sentiment delivered with an earnest smile. The fare is £2.50. I put in three and the machine keeps my change. We roar away towards Rumney Hill. Almost immediately Keyvan is reciting. This is from my book, *Words From The Heart*, he says, launching into a rhythmically fractured but spirited support of the Palestinian cause. We rattle past the Carpenters Arms towards Llanrumney. Keyvan is rhyming heavily about tears and fears, love and loss. The bus stops outside St Mellons to let on a shaking ancient on sticks. You're ninety-two, aren't you, says Keyvan, expecting no argument. Yes, I am, replies the pensioner. We thunder on. Keyvan takes a hand from the wheel to pull a wallet full of typed verse from his inside uniform pocket. I hang determinedly to the front grab handle, worried we might lurch straight across the approaching roundabout. This is a big bus and we are at full throttle. But Keyvan is well in control. I wrote this one for my aunty, he informs me. With one eye on the road and the other on his text we continue to move. When they escaped from Persia at the time of Khomeini's revolution, Keyvan's father wanted his son to become a nuclear physicist and enrolled him at University in Brighton. New world, new beginning. But the plan didn't work. I wanted to do what I wanted to do, Keyvan insists. You can think when you drive buses. I came here. Everyone knows me now. I publish my books. They go all over the world.

Outside Newport three schoolgirls wave their arms from an isolated shelter. Keyvan momentarily breaks from his recitation to dispense their tickets. Here, look at this. He produces a cutting from Newport's evening paper, *The South Wales Argus*, in which his photo smiles. The story is about his books, his bus driving and his work for charity. Keyvan Ghaemmaghami's verse may not be high art but it's literature to that great swath of the population who think of poetry as something that comes inside greetings cards. Poetry makes nothing happen, said Auden. Ghaemmaghami artlessly proves him wrong. Take a poll among Argus readers. Not that many in Newport would be able to suggest R.S. or Gillian Clarke as among Wales's pre-eminent but they'd all be able to name Ghaemmaghami. Our bus driver has no great literary pretensions. He is simply following compulsion.

We get to Newport Bus Station and because of Keyvan's enthusi-astic rattling I haven't seen anything of the city on the way in bar a sign still reading TOWN CENTRE glimpsed on a road island. Newport is a city now, in spirit if not in size. Its new status awarded under some Golden Jubilee dispensation. The buses already have the words CITY CENTRE on their destination boards. No union jacks visible apart from the set at the top of Commercial Road put up outside the Irish Club. The place doesn't care. Reaching Commercial Street I see two middle-aged bus-spotters noting arrivals. One has a shoulder-bag nerdily strapped diagonally across his chest. He holds his hands behind his back Duke of Edinburgh style rising rhythmically onto tip toe and then sinking back. His companion wears a coach enthusiasts convention sweat shirt with a print of bus on its front. He is taking notes. A bunch of teenagers in ripped jeans and with coloured hair smoke and stumble around the preserved 0-6-0 Pannier Tank engine now stuck on a grass verge. The Bus Station is ninety-sixties concrete grim – a gritty spread of bus bays, shelter, toilets, news-stands, gum blotched paving, and grime. Traditionally you arrive at cities through the worst doors they can offer. Newport's has

the expected complement of alcoholics and ragged no-hopers stretched out along its forecourt. More threatening than Cardiff, less light, an environment unrelieved by wealth of any sort. Newport is a working town. Used to be. Was. Steel, coal, docks. Closed or closing. Labour with little now to do. LG's semiconductor plants on the outskirts were the Korean tiger's life raft when they were built a few years back. But 6,000 jobs vanished in a synaptical crack as the bottom fell out of high tech. Next year the work will be back. Newport lives in hope.

If you believe the local historians Newport should have been called Gwynllwg after the chief who first camped on Stow Hill when the town was no more than a hut in a field. Or maybe Novus Burgus[1], which is what Giraldus Cambrensis called it. Or even Newcastle, which is what the place is called in Welsh – *Castell newydd ar Wysc*[2] – the new castle on the Usk – Casnewydd. But instead it's Newport after the port which grew around the flooding pill and marshy meadows where the Ebbw reached the Usk and the two poured on into the tidal Severn. Before 1800 Newport had a population of barely a thousand. In fifty years that grew to 70,000. Another testimony to the industrial revolution's rampant gargantuanism. Multiplying amoeba had nothing on nineteenth century south Wales, fired by iron, powered by coal, fed by the catholic Irish and tough south-west Englanders. Scene, in 1839, of the failed Chartist uprising against the British state. Half the rioters from England. Newport, Monmouthshire, Royal shire, left out of the Act of Union. Never sure which country it really belongs to. Welsh now in fact, but still at heart vaguely uncertain.

John Briggs, the Minnesotan, from the same mould as Clark Gable, grey haired, Tesco-bag carrying, appears from behind the newsstand. The pubs are not far, he says, and they are not. Barely a minute through the darkening streets and we find ourselves in the Windsor Castle. One of the few places left that sell real beer, a last haunt of the Bass drinker, Briggs tells me. A Wetherspoons opens and in the early weeks offers an exciting range of real ale but you know it won't last long. Newport's preference for the pasteurised will soon make its mark. The Windsor Castle has an original collection of wall decoration. Between ancient prints showing Dickensian scenes from The Old Curiosity Shop or French nineteenth century bourgeoisie society are advertisements for the Windsor Castle's

burgeoning gastronomic enterprise. New – Corned Beef Hash
Served With Chips and Peas – £2.99. Fantastic Food Offers – Jumbo
Sausages at £2.99. We stick to Bass.

John's view is that Newport's industrial decline mirrors that of
Cardiff, albeit on a smaller scale. Newport's two Alexandra Docks
were once outnumbered by Cardiff's Bute powered five. Yet today
both of Newport's still operate while at Cardiff things have been
significantly shut down. The essential difference between the two
ports is that Newport held onto its industry for longer. The giant
steelworks at nearby Llanwern, Western-world state of the art in the
sixties and many times the size of Cardiff's East Moors, have only
just closed. Newport is yet to be regenerated on any scale. Peter
Fink's red-painted *Steel Wave*, a twisted girder art work on the river
side in the town centre, remains a controversial commemoration of
Newport's steel trade. Derided when it went up in 1990, this is not
art this is scrap metal, used by the Borough ten years on as a symbol
of the town's moderness, disliked now for what it recalls.

When it's time to go and we've experienced the expected working-
class sights of middle-aged solo beer drinkers staring silently into
space; youths with bright red glasses of flavoured lager sending text
messages to each other across the tables; and women of a certain age
tapping us for cigarettes and free drinks I head off. I could have been
leaving Cardiff's Riverside. Crossing the pedestrianised centre to
where I've arranged a lift takes me past the mall stores, same here as
anywhere in the UK. M&S, BHS, Top Shop, Curry's, Dixon's, WH
Smith. Glass and mannequin. Racked TVs. Shelves and socks. But
somehow these Newport streets are different – a bit narrower, darker,
slightly uneven. Scratched by municipal repair, blocked by stacked
paving, too many planters. This built environment is the footprint of
an unfulfilled aspiration. Is this Wales or still the ragged edge of
England? Is this dark city going anywhere? The rain drifts in from the
south West, the fog of piddling mist that knocks the light and breath
from outdoor living. A couple of figures up ahead of me disappear
into a doorway. The guy sleeping in Boots entrance pulls himself in
out of the damp wind. An Asda carrier billows past to fly up out of
sight. Right now Newport is simply getting itself together. The future
is next. Any moment now Newport will be heading there.

CARDIFF, NEW YORK STATE

There are ten Cardiffs in the USA, plus one Cardiff-by-the-Sea. They are in Alabama, Colorado, Idaho, Illinois, Maryland, New Jersey, Pennsylvania, Tennessee, Texas and New York. The one by the sea is in California, named after the wife of its founder who came from Wales. We are visiting Cardiff, New York. It's upstate. Getting there isn't difficult, assuming of course that your starting point is not New York City itself but Syracuse, near the Canadian border at the Great Lakes. You follow Interstate 81 south to Scranton and take a left onto the 20 at LaFayette. We do it in Grahame Davies's rented Pontiac. The deep green forested hillsides we pass through look for all the world like the approaches to Merthyr. New York's Cardiff turns out not to be much. We miss it at our first pass and have to turn back at Tully. The road sign is overhung with foliage. The humidity here is high and the temperature is in the 80s. Two construction workers stand smoking next to a section of pipeline they are laying below the highway. You can hear blue jays and cat birds in the paper birch. In Cardiff itself – two streets, a graveyard, a Methodist church, a line of wooden shingle fronts – there's no one about.

We come here – Lloyd Robson, Grahame Davies and myself, all poets with the Welsh capital somewhere in our works – because this Cardiff has to have a connection with our Cardiff. It couldn't be the other way about, could it? On the Amtrak earlier, clacking up from Albany, an old man in a faded suit had got on at Utica. He'd asked where we came from and when told smiled. "I'm from there too –

Walesville." The Welsh must have got this far. I check the map. There's a Port Byron, a Lewis, a Newport, and even a Bangor. But no Llanfairfechan. Actually no Llan anything. Not here.

This Cardiff is in Onondaga County. The Onondaga are one of the Six Native American Nations. The firekeepers of the Iroquois. They made treaty with the white man early.

There's an Onondaga reservation smothered by white pine about four miles back down the highway. If you weren't looking for it then you wouldn't see it. The road sign is daubed with graffiti. *Welcome to Onondaga Reservation, where traitors, rapists and murderers rule.*[3] Other than with their trade in duty-free cigarettes Onondagan and local do not mix well. Corruption, arson, and tax evasion have upset the peace. Cardiff was once their land, used to be. Now it's not.

Walking along Cardiff's main street in the heat haze is surreal. The church tower with its clapboard clock plays a recording of 'I Need Thee Every Hour' – at a quarter to. It's like being at home, although this isn't a Welsh hymn, as everyone thinks, but actually composed by Annie Hawks of Cincinnati, in 1872. A shooting break pulls into the spacious Methodist car park, the only vehicle visible in Cardiff apart from our own. A middle-aged woman gets out and starts unloading flowers into the church's side-door. Other than for a Christening this, apparently, is as lively these days as things get.

It wasn't always so. Back in 1869 the place buzzed with thousands of visitors daily, travelling up from the big city to view the Giant. This was the Cardiff Giant, a ten-and-a-half foot tall petrified humanoid discovered by workmen digging a well in swampy ground behind Stub Newell's barn. Its arrival was well timed. The mid-nineteenth century in America had been one of great intellectual debate. Darwin's *The Origin of Species* had recently been published. The land was full of hell-fire fundamentalists determined to prove him wrong. Stub Newell and his brother-in-law, George Hull, were quick to capitalise. They erected a tent around the uncovered Giant where it lay in its pit, and began charging 50c for a fifteen minute viewing. Visitors came in droves. Special transports were run from Syracuse and other outlying towns. A gingerbread and sweet cider stall opened. Stub Newell erected a shed selling warm meals, oysters and oats. The big stone man was proving more popular than baseball.

What most of these fervent believers did not know was that the

Giant had actually been carved in Chicago. It was made from a large chunk of gypsum and had been carted under cover of darkness to Stub's farm by George Hull a year earlier. The colossus had then been buried surreptitiously in the marsh near Onondaga Creek to await its discovery. In its manufacture Hull had paid enormous attention to detail. Modelling the giant on himself its form was entirely human. Pores in the skin had been added by hammering the gypsum with darning needle-filled mallets. Great age had been simulated by scouring the surface with sand-packed sponges and then dousing with sulphuric acid. And all was o so secret. Hull's two sculptors had been paid extra to keep their mouths very shut.

Visitors split into two camps. The larger group were the petrefactionists who believed the Giant to be a fossilised man. As the Bible told, Giants had indeed walked the land in those days. God's word had been made real before their eyes. Their opposition, the pragmatists, were convinced that the Giant was in fact a millennia-old carving. Egypt would have nothing on this newly discovered North American wonder and the ancient civilisation it foretold. News of the Cardiff Giant went around the world.

Being astute in an age when if you weren't you died Hull and Newton took their profits early and sold the Giant on to a consortium of local entrepreneurs. It was moved from tiny Cardiff to a bigger stage in Syracuse and then on to Albany, Boston and finally New York where even larger numbers of visitors flocked to experience the wonder. But as with all things larger than life suspicion was just around the corner. Scientists, convinced that human flesh could never petrify whole, sought and eventually found evidence of manufacture. Marks on the Giant's surface when examined close-up were found to be consistent with those made by cold chisel. In addition the gypsum rock from which the Giant was composed was discovered not have deteriorated as it should have in the damp earth of Newell's farm. The Giant just couldn't be real. When pressed Hull and Newton admitted the scam.

Despite being exposed as a hoax, visitors to the Giant still came. The great showman, B.T. Barnum, never willing to let a good thing pass and unable to buy into the original, (although he did try, offering $15,000) had his own replica made out of wood. Gypsum and wood Giants were exhibited side by side at the World's Fair. Perversely the Barnum fake drew more visitors than the Hull original.

In the century that followed interest in the Cardiff Giant waned and the statue was variously boxed, stored and sold-on. It came to rest, somewhat incongruously, at the home of American baseball in Cooperstown, NY. At the Farmer's Museum there, a sort of St Fagans of early Americana with keepers dressed in style with their exhibits, the Giant once again lies in a pit and is surrounded by a replica of George Hull's viewing tent. This time it costs $8 to get in. The two women in the line in front of me, from Michigan, wearing hats and slacks, say they'd never have been convinced. The Giant's penis looks far too small. They don't actually say this but I'm sure it's what they're thinking. At the bookshop the matronly owner asks me where I'm from. I'm buying a Cardiff Giant fridge magnet, six Cardiff Giant postcards and a set of Cardiff Giant coasters. Ideal Christmas presents, I reckon. "Cardiff," I say, "the other one." "And where exactly is that," she asks, "some folks were in here the other day enquiring and I just couldn't recall." I tell her. Wales. "Well, you don't say. My people were from there, on my mother's side. Wales, huh. Never been there myself. Guess now I never will."

Back in Cardiff, NY, the graveyard refuses to give up any Welsh names. We've got Bailey, Garfield, McIntire, Parkerson, Abbott, Sniffen, Sherman, Wescott, Winchell. Not one Williams. No Jones. No Davies. There's a Morgan but I could be misreading that. Here lies William W. Williams, Pontcanna, who founded Cardiff, NY, in 1825. That's the headstone I want to find. But the truth is much more prosaic. In 1839 one John F. Card built a grist mill not far from the village of LaFayette. He was a good guy, opened a store and a distillery, and people settled just to be near. They wanted their emerging township to have its own identity to mark it as a place different from the rest of the world. They wanted to name it after their provider of work, goods and alcohol, Mr Card. Cardbury and Cardville didn't sound right so Cardiff it became. A Welsh echo among the slowly rolling Onondaga hills. "No one frets about the name", says the Rev Beachamp in his local history, "It might have been worse".

Cardiff Could Be:

Cardiff, Alabama, Jefferson County, Pop 72
Cardiff, Colorado, Garfield County
Cardiff, Idaho, Clearwater County
Cardiff, Illinois, Livingston County
Cardiff, Maryland, Harford County
Cardiff, New Jersey, Atlantic County
Cardiff, New York, Onondaga County
Cardiff, Pennsylvania, Cambria County
Cardiff, Tennessee, Roane County
Cardiff, Texas, Waller County
Cardiff By the Sea, California, San Diego County,
Pop 11,781, near Cottonwood Creek, full of sun
Cardiff, NSW, Australia
Walton Cardiff, Gloucester, rain
Cardiff, ten miles from Newport, Pembs
Suburb of Bristol
Dark side of the moon
Sands of Mars

notes

1. Latin – Giraldus Cambrensis, 1191
2. Brut Y Tywysogion, 1400
3. Put there – I'm told – by Onondagans rather than white locals. Internecine strife.

THE PHOTOGRAPHS

All photographs by Peter Finch, apart from p194, Sue Wiltshire.

WORKS CONSULTED

Abse, Dannie, *The Two Roads Taken*, Enitharmon, 2003

Bala, Iwan, *here + now*, Seren, 2003

Borden, Iain and Dunster, David (editors), *Architecture And The Sites Of History*, Whitney, 1995

Breverton, Terry, *Glamorgan Seascape Pathways*. Wales Books, 2003

City of Cardiff Parks Dept., *Take A Walk In The Park – Cefn On Walk*, City of Cardiff, 1970

Carradice, Phil, *Penarth Pier 1894-1994*. Baron, 1994

Crickhowell, Nicholas, *Opera House Lottery – Zaha Hadid and the Cardiff Bay Project*, University of Wales Press, 1997

Friends of Nant Fawr Woodlands, *The Nant Fawr Woodlands – A Community Treasure*, City of Cardiff, 2001

Gillham, Mary E., A *Natural History of Cardiff. Exploring Along The River Taff*. Lazy Cat Publishing, 2002

Gillham, Mary E., *The Garth Countryside. Part of Cardiff's Green Mantle*. Lazy Cat Publishing, 1999

Green, Jonathon, *Days In the Life. Voices from the English Undergrounds 1961-1971*. Pimlico, 1998

Hilling, John B, *Cardiff and the Valleys – Architecture and Townscape*, Lund Humphries, 1973

Hodge, John, *The South Wales Main Line Part One – Cardiff*, Wild Swan Publications, 2003

Jenkins, Nigel, *Footsore On the Frontier*, Gomer 2001

Museum of Welsh Life Visitor Guide. NMGW, 2001

Newman, John, *The Buildings Of Wales – Glamorgan*, Penguin Books, 1995

North, Geoffrey A., *The Archive Photographs Series – Penarth and Sully*, Chalford 1998

Parker, Matthew & Carter, Nicholas, *Bute Town A Visitor's Guide*, Survey of Cardiff Occasional Paper No 2, 1989

Perkins, John W., *The Building Stones Of Cardiff – Geological Trail Guides*, University College Cardiff Press, 1984

Pilcher, Barry Edgar, and Williams, Mark, *Magic City*, Speed Limit Publications, 1977

Robins, Gary, *Prefabrications. Newport's Temporary Bungalows. The First Fifty Years*, Ffotogallery, 2001

Rowson, Stephen and Wright, Ian L., *The Glamorganshire and Aberdare Canals Vol 1*, Black Dwarf Publications, 2001

Salter, Ben, *Penarth – Official Town Guide*, Kenrich Publications, 2003

Sinclair, Neil M.C., *Endangered Tiger – A Community Under Threat*, Butetown History & Arts Centre, 2003

Super Red Book Cardiff, Estate Publications, 2001

Thomas, Huw, *Discovering Cities – Cardiff*. Geographical Association, 2003

Thorne, Alan – *Place Names Of Penarth – Historical and Colloquial* – D Brown & Sons, 1997

Tilney, Chrystal, *The Archive Photographs Series – Dinas Powys, St Andrews Major and Michaelson-Le-Pit*, Chalford 1996

Tripp, John, *Collected Poems 1958-78* – Christopher Davies, 1978

Williams, Stewart (Editor), *The Cardiff Book*, Stewart Williams, Publishers, 1973

Williams, Stewart (Editor), *South Glamorgan A County History*, Stewart Williams, Publishers, 1975

See also the list included in *Real Cardiff* #1.

INDEX

THE AUTHOR

Peter Finch is a poet, author and critic who lives in Cardiff. His numerous poetry titles include *Useful*, *Poems for Ghosts* and *Food* from Seren, and *Antibodies* from Stride. A selection of his work appeared in Hungarian translation as *Water / Vizet* in 2003. He has written a number of books on the business of writing including *How To Publish Yourself* (Allison & Busby) and *The Poetry Business* (Seren). He compiles the poetry section for Macmillan's annual *Writer's Handbook* and the self-publishing section for A&C Black's *Writers' & Artists' Yearbook*. His extensive website can be viewed at www.peterfinch.co.uk. A former publisher and bookseller, he is Chief Executive of Yr Academi Gymreig / The Welsh Academy, the Welsh National Literature Promotion Agency and Society of Writers.

Real Cardiff #1 which appeared in 2002 was a best seller. Peter Finch is currently editor for Seren's *Real Wales* series and, with Grahame Davies, has compiled *The Big Book of Cardiff*, an anthology of poetry and prose which concentrates on the revitalised city.

THE CRITICS ON REAL CARDIFF

This is a marvellous book – one of the very best books about a city I have ever read. It makes me feel terribly old-fashioned – superficial too, because I have never actually lived in the cities I have written about. I skip most of the poems, which I don't understand, but everything else in it is gripping me so fast that I have momentarily suspended my first ever reading of *Wuthering Heights*.

Jan Morris

Native Cardiffians now have the definitive guide to their city... the excitement of being one of the newest European capitals hangs light in the air.

Kate Nicholson
Writers' News

A wealth of information on the significance of familiar sites for those who live in Cardiff and an interesting insight into Wales' capital for those who don't, *Real Cardiff* is far more indicative of life in the city than the average tourist guide.

Cathryn Scott
The Big Issue

Every district is covered and there is something new to discover in every section. This will be a best seller and will be the top gift on my Christmas present list this year!

Bill Barrett
Cardiff Post

The travel section of the *Observer* highlights Wales as a 'place to visit' in 2003. If you are persuaded, and would like a genuine flavour of the capital, read Peter Finch, who has studied the city in historical depth and quartered it on foot and will entertain you all the way.

Sam Adams

The book's great strength is not in the macro but in the micro, in the deep, prolonged engagement with a particular place which has produced a richly nuanced, affectionate and sometimes exasperated portrait of a city. The beauty lies in the detail.

Grahame Davies
New Welsh Review

Cunningly intermeshed with this cornucopia of useful and fascinating material is an account of how a young man who was something or other in the City Hall became an editor, a publisher, a bookseller, an arts administrator and a poet – the most surreally inventive and provocative writer we have – without leaving the city's limits.

Meic Stephens
Cambria

This book should be read by anyone who wants to get to know more about Cardiff. That should include most people in Wales for a start. Even the ones in places like Swansea, Aberystwyth and Caernarfon.

Raymond Humphreys
Cambrensis

Lurking behind much of the text is a reassurance from Peter Finch to the reader, and from Peter Finch to himself, that the poet's place is that of an outsider, even when the poet in question has become, ostensibly at least, part of the Establishment. And that's why the subject matter fits so well. Cardiff, that deeply self-conscious and not-very-Welsh capital of Wales, that country with more chips than Barry island, is truly the outsider's metropolis.

Mike Parker
Planet